OECD Reviews of Vocational Education and Training

Vocational Education and Training in Estonia

Pauline Musset, Simon Field, Anthony Mann and Benedicte Bergseng

This work is published under the responsibility of the Secretary-General of the OECD. The opinions expressed and arguments employed herein do not necessarily reflect the official views of OECD member countries.

This document, as well as any data and any map included herein, are without prejudice to the status of or sovereignty over any territory, to the delimitation of international frontiers and boundaries and to the name of any territory, city or area.

Please cite this publication as:
Musset, P., et al. (2019), *Vocational Education and Training in Estonia*, OECD Reviews of Vocational Education and Training, OECD Publishing, Paris.
https://doi.org/10.1787/g2g9fac9-en

ISBN 978-92-64-31308-8 (print)
ISBN 978-92-64-31309-5 (pdf)

OECD Reviews of Vocational Education and Training
ISSN 2077-7728 (print)
ISSN 2077-7736 (online)

The statistical data for Israel are supplied by and under the responsibility of the relevant Israeli authorities. The use of such data by the OECD is without prejudice to the status of the Golan Heights, East Jerusalem and Israeli settlements in the West Bank under the terms of international law.

Photo credits: Cover © LituFalco - Fotolia.com.

Corrigenda to OECD publications may be found on line at: *www.oecd.org/about/publishing/corrigenda.htm.*

Foreword

Estonia has experienced extensive reform in its vocational education and training (VET) system in recent years. As a result, Estonia's VET system is very well-designed: the engagement of employers is strong, in particular through a system of occupational qualification and standards, which underpins the development of programmes. About 25% of students at the upper secondary level are enrolled in a vocational programme, delivered by 30 different VET providers. There is a relatively new apprenticeship system that is growing quickly. Educational and labour market outcomes are also good: young Estonians do extremely well on the Programme for International Student Assessment (PISA) and the Survey of Adult Skills (PIAAC), and unemployment rates are very low. Despite Estonia's efforts in reforming their VET system, however, some concerns remain. This OECD review assesses both the strengths of the Estonian VET system and the challenges it faces, making proposals for how those challenges might be addressed.

Chapter 1 provides an overview of Estonian VET reform and the remaining challenges. Compared to the general education route offered by upper secondary selective institutions and higher education institutions, VET is perceived as low social status. In order to be more attractive, it needs to improve its offer to those who wish to pursue higher level technical skills and allow progression into further learning opportunities. Dropout rates remain high and few young people choose the apprenticeship route.

Chapter 2 recommends the expansion of work-based learning within VET programmes and youth apprenticeships, and the separation of upper secondary institutions from basic schools, to remove the risks of bias in the decisions of students on whether to pursue general education or VET. It also proposes measures to tackle dropout, including financial incentives to institutions and targeted support in numeracy and literacy. Chapter 3 recommends improving pathways between VET and other programmes, including those delivered by higher education institutions, and further action to enhance equity in provision in order to ensure fair access to post-secondary and higher education by gender, region and mother tongue. These approaches should be designed to attract into VET more students with good school performance, and raise the status of VET in general. Chapter 4 recommends improving career guidance, making some elements of it mandatory before grade 9, for all schools and all students.

This report was drafted by Pauline Musset, Simon Field, Anthony Mann and Benedicte Bergseng, with the OECD Centre for Skills overseeing the final draft. Elisa Larrakoetxea and Jennifer Cannon provided valuable administrative support. The OECD is very grateful to all the hundreds of people throughout Estonia who gave their time to take part in meetings with the visiting OECD team and contributed their knowledge and ideas to this exercise. Particular thanks are owed to Katrin Rein, Helen Põllo and Anneli Roose from the Ministry of Education and Research, who were most directly involved in facilitating the work of the OECD and the missions, and Kaie Piiskop and Kersti Raudsepp from Foundation Innove, for an excellent background report. The OECD also wants to thank the European Commission for their support, in particular Mantas Sekmokas and Dana-Carmen Bachmann.

Within the OECD, Anthony Mann supported the preparation of this report as head of the Vocational Education and Training (VET) and Adult Learning team within the OECD Centre for Skills, overseeing the final draft. The report benefited from many helpful comments and advice from Cécile Bily and Tanja Bastianić from the OECD Directorate for Education and Skills and Caroline Klein and Zuzana Smidova from the Economics Department. Support throughout the exercise was received from Montserrat Gomendio as head of the Centre for Skills, Dirk van Damme as head of the Skills beyond School Division, Andreas Schleicher, Director of the Directorate for Education and Skills and Stefano Scarpetta, Director of the Directorate for Employment. Labour and Social Affairs.

This report has been co-funded by the European Union. The opinions expressed and arguments employed herein do not necessarily reflect the official views of the European Union or of the OECD member countries.

Table of contents

Tables

Figures

Boxes

Follow OECD Publications on:

http://twitter.com/OECD_Pubs

http://www.facebook.com/OECDPublications

http://www.linkedin.com/groups/OECD-Publications-4645871

http://www.youtube.com/oecdilibrary

http://www.oecd.org/oecddirect/

This book has...

StatLinks

A service that delivers Excel® files from the printed page!

Look for the *StatLinks* at the bottom of the tables or graphs in this book. To download the matching Excel® spreadsheet, just type the link into your Internet browser, starting with the *http://dx.doi.org* prefix, or click on the link from the e-book edition.

Executive summary

Introduction

Over the past years, the Estonian vocational education and training (VET) system has undergone extensive reforms and developments. Reforms have aimed to create a clearer and more effective qualifications system to enhance employer engagement, to consolidate the school network and improve school facilities, to increase work-based learning and develop apprenticeship, and to meet the needs of both young people and adults in a framework of lifelong learning. Effective arrangements are in place to prepare teachers of vocational subjects. Basic school outcomes, as measured by the Programme for International Student Assessment (PISA), are outstanding, and participation in upper secondary education is near-universal. These are impressive achievements. But challenges remain in improving the status of the VET system so as it can raise to its potential in the skills system of a rapidly changing economy, and in overcoming equity challenges. This report assesses the strengths of the Estonian VET system, the challenges it faces, and makes proposals for how those challenges could be addressed.

Developing the foundations of the VET system

In Estonia, only around one quarter of young people enter an upper secondary vocational track – a lower proportion than in many comparable OECD countries. Around 150 schools in Estonia provide general education in all 12 grades, offering a default option for young people in their ninth grade to remain in the same school, and therefore in general education, for their upper secondary school. A separation of the upper secondary school system from basic schooling would help to remove this bias, so that all ninth-grade students would face a real choice between VET and general education. Co-operation, and where practical at the local level, mergers between general academic and vocational upper secondary schools should be promoted.

While dropout rates have fallen, they remain too high in vocational upper secondary programmes, with around one-quarter of entrants failing to complete. One useful step, implementing recommendations of the 2016 OECD school resources review of Estonia, would be to link some school funding to completions.

A promising apprenticeship system has been launched in Estonia, but apprentice numbers, although increasing, remain low and limited to adults. Given its potential, renewed attempts to develop youth apprenticeship are needed, by focusing for example on a specific region and/or industry and considering specific employer incentives. In other vocational programmes, work practice in enterprises can be introduced as a formal and mandatory requirement.

There are large differences in participation rates in upper secondary VET for young people coming from different socio-economic backgrounds – for example in eastern Estonia, around 60% of Russian-speaking boys enrol in the VET track, while in the larger cities, only 10% of Estonian-speaking girls do so. While variations are monitored, policy responses are undeveloped. The Estonian authorities should explore with stakeholders potential responses to large disparities to ensure that all Estonians can realise their career and learning potential.

Pathways and progression

The aspiration to higher education is now nearly universal. For young people, the perception of academic upper secondary education as the natural route to university offers formidable competition to any parallel vocational track. In Estonia as elsewhere, this means that initial vocational education must be a first step to lifelong learning, and not a dead end.

For initial VET graduates in Estonia, many learning pathways are open in principle, but rarely travelled. The optional extra year of education that helps upper secondary VET graduates to qualify for higher education attracted only 21 students in 2016. The vast majority of entrants to higher education and post-secondary programmes of all types have graduated from upper secondary general education, rather than VET.

This is a major challenge, since the prospect of progression is often the key tool to attract good candidates into the VET track. A multi-dimensional strategy is needed to facilitate progression from initial VET, working across the education system, ensuring that career guidance addresses progression beyond VET, establishing a dialogue with higher education institutions to encourage interest in candidates from VET backgrounds, developing frameworks of credit recognition and addressing equity issues.

Within upper secondary VET, a hybrid programme might be usefully developed, leading both to a VET qualification and to the state examination that normally gives access to higher education. Such a programme could draw on successful hybrid models implemented in other countries such as Denmark, and would be able to attract into VET high performing students who might otherwise not consider the option.

In addition, Estonia should develop its already strong professional examination system to encourage upper secondary VET graduates to upskill, possibly with additional financial support. Some consideration should also be given to using a central fund, as in the model of higher VET developed in Sweden, to address sectoral and regional skills shortages and reskilling needs.

Strengthening career guidance

In a rapidly evolving labour market, navigating a path of learning and work is increasingly challenging. Good quality career guidance and information is therefore vital to young people (and adults) to ensure that they make the right choices. In Estonia, career guidance and information services have been extensively reorganised, and the system now has many strengths, but some gaps remain.

Some of the elements of career guidance should be made mandatory in basic schools and provision should start earlier, ensuring all students speak to impartial and independent career advisers. Mandatory provision helps to ensure that the guidance gets through to the students who need it most. This in itself would provide a firmer foundation for decisions about whether to pursue a VET or general education track. More accessible and understandable labour market information, including data from destinations surveys, would also be very helpful.

Young people can also benefit from being in contact with people from different professional backgrounds and from visits to actual workplaces, and activities such as short work placements and work shadowing.

Chapter 1. Overview: Reforms and challenges in the Estonian vocational education and training system

Estonia's education system has many impressive achievements: the Programme for International Student Assessment (PISA) results are outstanding and participation in upper secondary education is near-universal. But challenges remain in particular in the country's vocational education and training (VET) system. This chapter gives an overview of Estonia's education system, as well as developments in the economy and in the labour market. Against this background, it analyses the VET system, and assesses both its strengths and challenges, which provides the structure for the rest of the report.

The statistical data for Israel are supplied by and under the responsibility of the relevant Israeli authorities. The use of such data by the OECD is without prejudice to the status of the Golan Heights, East Jerusalem and Israeli settlements in the West Bank under the terms of international law.

Introduction

Reforms of the VET system in Estonia are impressive, but challenges remain

Recent years have witnessed extensive reform of the Estonian vocational education and training (VET) system. The qualifications system has been transformed, and occupational standards, agreed with employers, now underpin vocational qualifications. The VET school network has been re-organised, and facilities modernised. The mix of provision is now increasingly guided by the OSKA system for identifying labour force needs. A new level 5 VET qualification has been introduced. An apprenticeship system was established in 2006 and, most recently, a strategy for lifelong learning has been developed in which VET provision is nested. These, alongside a wide range of further reforms, are impressive achievements. But challenges remain in improving the status of the VET system, so that it can play a fuller part in meeting the needs of a fast-growing and changing economy, and helping to overcome the equity challenges that Estonia still faces.

This report assesses the Estonian VET system

This report assesses the strengths of the Estonian VET system, the challenges it faces, and makes proposals for how those challenges might be addressed. The report rests on a background report provided by Estonia describing the VET system, and two study missions to Estonia in April and June 2017 by OECD teams, involving discussions with a wide variety of stakeholders. It also draws extensively on the OECD's range of data, knowledge and experience of the vocational education and training systems of other countries as well as in Estonia (Box 1.1).

This first chapter aims to set the scene

This chapter briefly summarises developments in the economy and labour market of Estonia, and describes the education system. Against that background, it looks at the VET system, assessing its strengths, the challenges that remain, and summarises the suggestions for policy advanced in later chapters of the report. The three chapters which follow look at the main challenges in different areas, advance policy recommendations and set out arguments in support. Chapter 2 looks at the foundations of the VET system in initial VET programmes, mainly for young people. Chapter 3 examines subsequent pathways for VET graduates. Chapter 4 looks at how young people choose their preferred pathways, and whether they have enough information and guidance to make good choices.

Box 1.1. OECD reviews of vocational education and training

In a sequence of more than 50 country studies, the OECD has been reviewing vocational education systems around the world since 2007. Two major reports drawing together the policy lessons from this very large range of international experience – these are *Learning for Jobs,* published in (2010[1]), and *Skills beyond School* published in (2014[2]).

The country studies cover Australia, Austria, Belgium (Flanders), Canada, Chile, China (People's Republic of), Costa Rica, the Czech Republic, Denmark, Egypt, Germany, Hungary, Iceland, Ireland, Israel, Kazakhstan, Korea, Mexico, the Netherlands, Norway, Romania, Slovak Republic, Spain, Sweden, South Africa, Switzerland, the United Kingdom, and the United States.

The country studies are available online: www.oecd.org/education/innovation-education/vet.htm.

The wider economic context

The economy is doing well

The global recession following the financial crisis had severe effects on Estonia, inducing sharp declines in employment and high rates of youth unemployment. Estonia has now recovered well as its economy and income levels are converging on the European and OECD average (OECD, 2017[3]). Labour market participation has regained high levels, and public finances are solid. Economic growth is increasing, and as a result, skill shortages are increasingly a challenge (see below). The unemployment rate at the end of 2017 at about 5%, was slightly below the OECD average, with a youth unemployment rate of 12%, again below the OECD average of 13% (OECD, 2018[4]).

But Estonia faces some significant equity challenges

High income inequality in Estonia stems from both inequality in labour market income and a tax-benefit system which has a limited redistributive effect. It leaves a considerable proportion of the population at risk of poverty, with risks significantly higher for the unemployed, and those with disabilities or little education, as in most OECD countries (OECD, 2017[3]). There are also specific issues facing the Russian-speaking minority and women.

The Russian-speaking minority face difficulties

Integration of the Russian-speaking minority (around 25% of the total population) in the labour market remains a challenge, particularly in the eastern regions of the country (OECD, 2015[5]). The unemployment rate of this minority is three percentage points higher than for all Estonians, partly explained by regional economic disparities. The most recent OECD economic survey recommends a whole-of-government approach to tackle the obstacles encountered by this minority, which include limited Estonian language skills and weaker social contacts and networks (OECD, 2017[3]).

Gender disparities are greater in Estonia than in many OECD countries

In Estonia, women have high employment rates and outperform men in the education system. However women earn on average 30% less than men, one of the largest wage gaps in the OECD, explained mostly by the difference in the distribution of employment across occupations and sectors between men and women (Anspa and Rõõm, 2007[6]; EU Skills Panorama, 2014[7]; Anspal, 2015[8]). Mothers with a child under three have relatively low employment rates by the standards of other OECD countries, reflecting the very long periods of parental leave available to Estonian mothers (OECD, 2017[3]).

Some migrant workers are starting to return

Emigration from Estonia has been significant in previous years, and it has put pressure on the labour market, especially as the working age population is declining. Since 2015, an increase in return migration has taken place, reflecting Estonia's strong labour market (OECD, 2017[3]). It is estimated that 23 000 Estonian residents, or nearly 4% of employed persons, have previously worked abroad; two-thirds of which in Finland. Middle-aged men, usually with vocational secondary education and working in construction and transportation, form the largest group of cross-border workers (EU Skills Panorama, 2014[7]; Ministry of Education and Research, 2017[9]). Cross-border working has important benefits for the workers concerned, including wage gains as well as valuable experience and training abroad. Migrants' remittances also boost Estonian household incomes (OECD, 2015[5]).

Firms have recruitment difficulties, and Estonian workers are looking to upskill

While the economy is growing, Estonia's working-age population is declining. Despite fast-increasing wages, businesses complain about difficulties in recruiting skilled employees, particularly in certain sectors (World Economic Forum, 2016[10]; Eesti Pank, 2017[11]). Alongside the objective evidence, Estonian workers tend to see themselves as lacking skills. In 2014, around 40% of employees said in the European Working Conditions Survey that they had insufficient skills for their job at the time of hiring, one of the highest shares in the European Union. 30% of Estonian respondents said that they need more training to cope well with the duties at the job (Eurofound, 2015[12]). This is the highest level among the European countries participating in this survey.[1]

The education system of Estonia

The organisation of the education system

The strength of the Estonian education system has deep historical roots

In the late nineteenth century, census data shows that Estonia's literacy rate, at 94%, was the highest in the Tsardom of Russia – an indicator of the deep roots of modern education achievements (Estonica, 2018[13]). Estonia's current education system now reflects a long programme of reform since the end of the Soviet era (Lees, 2016[14]) and Estonia displays some of the highest rates of education attainment, and performance by 15-year-olds in the PISA tests of numeracy, literacy and scientific literacy, in the OECD.

Basic education links primary and lower secondary education in a single phase

Pre-school education is not compulsory and is generally provided at childcare institutions for one-and-a-half to seven-year-olds. Compulsory education, from age seven, includes nine years of basic education or until a learner reaches age 17. Usually primary and lower secondary education are grouped together in a single phase of education in basic schools, but primary education (grades 1 to 6) is sometimes also offered in separate schools, usually to ensure better accessibility for learners in rural areas.

Upper secondary education includes both a general education and a VET track

Although upper secondary education is not compulsory, nearly all students continue to that level, and Estonia has one of the highest rates of participation at this level in the OECD. In grade 9, students make a choice over whether to enter the vocational or general track, and three-quarters continue in general education. In some cases this involves no change of school because the students are in full-cycle schools offering all school grades, including the final three upper secondary grades as well as basic schooling. There were 149 such full-cycle schools in 2017. (The potential biases in decision-making created by such schools are further discussed in Chapter 2). Increasingly, partly because of the creation of new free-standing upper secondary general education schools, students have to change schools for this phase of education (Ministry of Education and Research, 2017[9]; CEDEFOP, 2017[15]).

Central government owns and manages most upper secondary schools

Most, but not all basic schools are owned and managed by municipalities. Some basic schools are also owned by private entities and some basic schools for Special Educational Needs (SEN) students are owned by central government. Most but not all upper secondary schools, both general (free-standing ones) and vocational, are owned and managed by central government.[2] There are a few exceptions where upper secondary VET institutions are managed by municipalities, or by private sector providers (CEDEFOP, 2017[15]).

There are both professional higher education institutions and universities

General upper secondary education completes with the state examination (mother tongue, mathematics and foreign language) which, although not a formal requirement, is used by most higher education institutions as a means of choosing entrants. Higher education is divided between professional higher education institutions and universities. They are accessible in principle to graduates of upper secondary education from both general and vocational tracks, but in practice entrants are overwhelmingly from general education (an issue considered in Chapter 3). A programme of consolidation has reduced the number of higher education institutions from 44 in 2005 to 21 in 2016. These include six state and one private universities, and eight state and six private professional higher education institutions (Lees, 2016[14]).

Attainment and basic skills

Only 12% of young adults have less than upper secondary qualifications

Looking at young adults, in 2016, only 12% of those aged 25-34 have less than upper secondary qualifications, well under the OECD average of 16%. 41% of these young adults have tertiary qualifications, only slightly less than the OECD average. Attainment rates in Estonia have been high for many years, so that unlike most OECD countries, tertiary attainment in the older generation is quite similar to that among young adults (OECD, 2018[16]).

Learning outcomes from basic school, in literacy, numeracy and science are outstanding

The most outstanding feature of Estonian education is not the attainment rates, but the evidence on learning outcomes. Estonia's performance on the PISA tests, is outstanding in reading, maths and science, with the best results in the whole of Europe, and among the best in world. It also scores very well in terms of equity, which means that socio-economic background has a smaller impact on performance than in other OECD countries (OECD, 2016[17]). But one outstanding equity challenge is the gap between Estonian and Russian speaking schools – the performance difference is estimated at one school year on the PISA test (Ministry of Education and Research, 2018[18]).

Figure 1.1. Only 18% of Estonian adults lack basic skills

Percentage of all adults aged 16-65

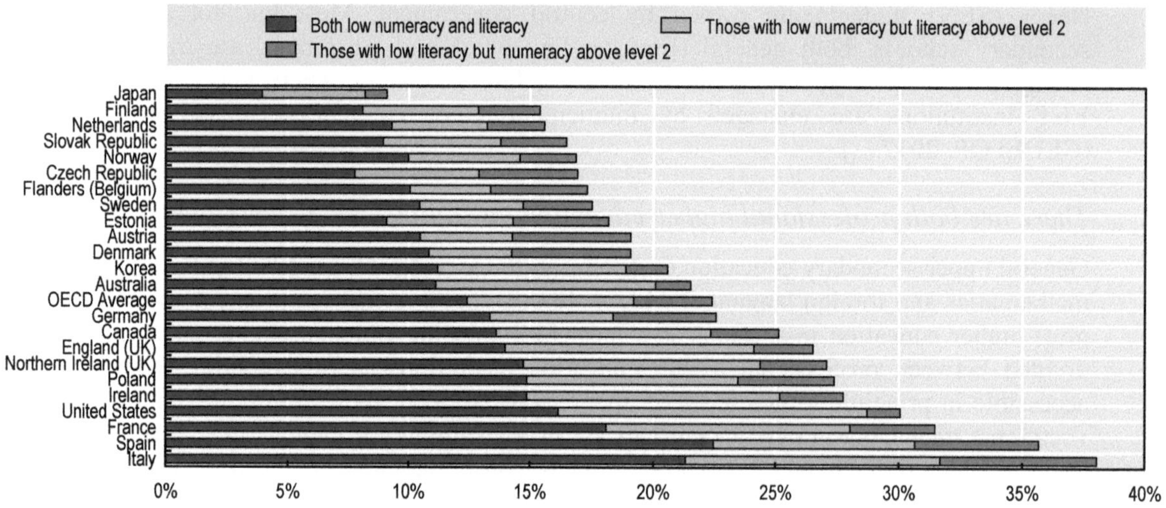

Source: Calculations based on OECD (2015[19]), OECD Survey of Adult Skills (PIAAC) (Database 2012, 2015), www.oecd.org/skills/piaac/publicdataandanalysis/.

StatLink ▄▄▆▆ https://doi.org/10.1787/888933921681

Skills of adults are also impressive

The Survey of Adult Skills, a product of the Programme for the International Assessment of Adult Competencies (PIAAC), shows that Estonian adults (16-65 year-olds) have very good literacy and numeracy skills, significantly above those in many other participating OECD countries and young adults (16-24 year-olds) do even better. Among adults as a whole, Estonia is ranked 7th for literacy and 11th for numeracy. Estonia is the OECD country with the lowest difference in literacy proficiency between adults with high and low educated parents. And at the lower end of the distribution the proportion of low-skilled adults (scoring under level 2) is relatively small at 18% (against an average of 22%) (Figure 1.1). About half of the low skilled are over 55.

11% of young people are neither employed nor in education or training (NEET)

Both educational attainment and basic skills influence the likelihood of becoming a NEET. In Estonia, 11% of 16-29 year-olds are NEET as are 24% of low-skilled 16-29 year-olds. Many NEETs are low skilled, and although Estonia compared relatively well to other countries; the situation is still worrying. Many NEETs also have low educational attainment, but not always (OECD, 2017[20]).

Estonia's vocational education and training system

While nearly all students continue in upper secondary education, only one-quarter choose VET

After completing basic school, about one-quarter (26%) of students enter VET programmes, while 70% of students enter upper secondary general education, proportions which have barely changed over recent years (Ministry of Education and Research, 2017[9]). This means that rather fewer young adults have vocational qualifications than in a number of other OECD countries where entry into the vocational track is more usual (Figure 1.2).

Figure 1.2. Relative to other countries, a smaller proportion of young Estonians have upper secondary VET as their highest qualification

Percentage of 16-40 year-olds with upper secondary VET as highest qualification

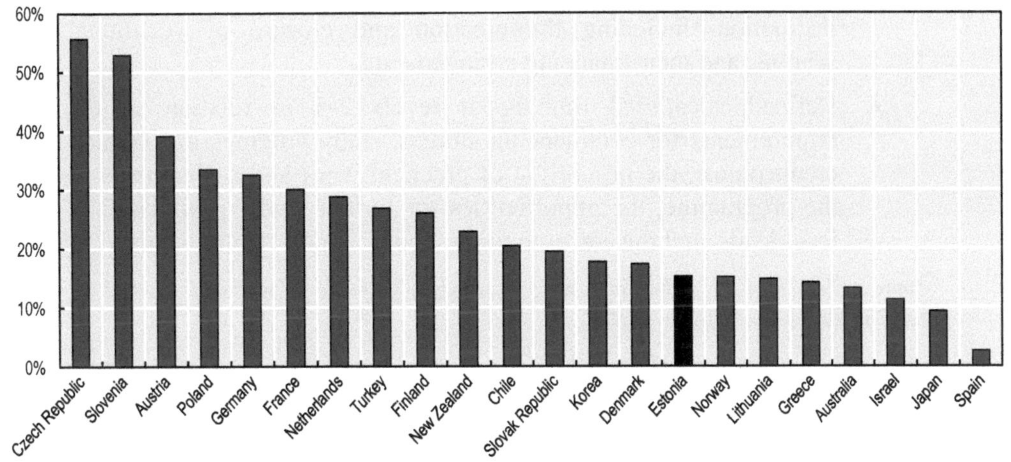

Note: Canada, England (United Kingdom), Flanders, Ireland, Italy, Northern Ireland (United Kingdom), Sweden and the United States were excluded from the analysis because of data issues.
Source: Calculations based on OECD (2015[19]), OECD Survey of Adult Skills (PIAAC) (Database 2012, 2015), www.oecd.org/skills/piaac/publicdataandanalysis/.

StatLink https://doi.org/10.1787/888933921700

Upper secondary VET programmes provide skills in a target occupation

Most students entering VET after basic education pursue an upper secondary VET programme at European Qualifications Framework (EQF) level 4, which includes both general and vocational education (ISCED 354). These programmes are mostly 3 years in length, some are 4, and typically lead to an occupational examination. State examinations, used by higher education institutions as a means to choosing entrants, are also available for upper secondary VET graduates as an option (CEDEFOP, 2017[15]), and can be taken the same year as completing the VET programme, or following an additional year of general education studies. Few students choose this latter option (Ministry of Education and Research, 2017[9]). A major reform of the Estonian VET system took place in 2013 and this is described in Box 1.2.

Box 1.2. The 2013 Vocational Educational Institutions Act

This legislation launched several reforms of vocational education and training in Estonia. The legislation:

- Defined some new categories of vocational training, directly linked to the Estonian qualifications framework. These included level 5 programmes for post-secondary vocational education and training.

- Re-established a framework for the right to provide vocational instruction, including the creation and closure of vocational schools, and their financing arrangements.

- Defined vocational training at levels 2-5 in relation to the requirements for commencing studies, study volumes in Estonian credit points, the proportion of practical work and assignments in the programme, the opportunities for further study to which each level leads, and the corresponding labour market requirements.

Source: Ministry of Education and Research (2018[21]), *Vocational Education*, https://www.hm.ee/en/activities/vocational-education.

There is also provision for adults

A second type of upper secondary VET at EQF level 4 excludes general education, and is usually pursued by adults seeking a particular occupational skill. Many of them already have a general upper secondary education qualification. Partly, but not entirely because of demographic change, adults are increasingly prominent among VET students, while the number of young learners is decreasing (Ministry of Education and Research, 2017[9]) (Figure 1.3).

Figure 1.3. The proportion of older VET students is increasing

Number of students in all VET programmes, by age

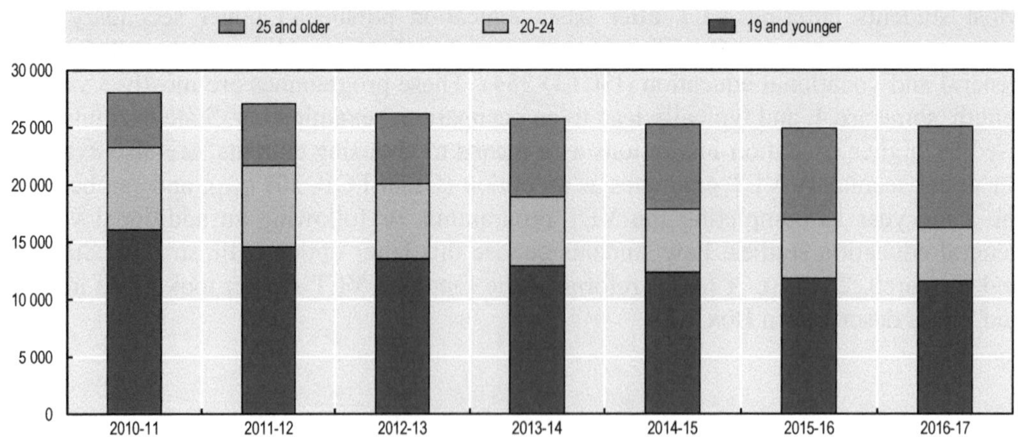

Source: Adapted from Ministry of Education and Research (2017[9]), *Background Report for OECD on Vocational Education and Training (VET) in Estonia*, www.hm.ee/sites/default/files/uuringud/oecd_vet_background.pdf

StatLink https://doi.org/10.1787/888933921719

VET schools are under different governance arrangements

Twenty-six VET institutions are under state administration, three under municipalities, and four are private. Municipalities and private schools can also fund education offers that they consider important and that have not been covered by state funding. Although largely government-owned, VET institutions have extensive autonomy. Funding is given to a broad curriculum group, rather than a single programme, and the school decides, within that broad heading, which programmes at which levels they will teach (Ministry of Education and Research, 2017[9]).

Post-secondary programmes are also available

Since 2013, students have been able to pursue VET EQF level 5 qualifications. These may be taken either as part of initial VET, or through continuous VET, with differences in the way the coursework is organised. The share of work-based learning (practical workshops at school and work practice at enterprises) is at least 50%. Professional higher education programmes (professional bachelors, level 6) can be pursued in one of the eight professional higher education institutions mentioned above. In the Estonian system, these programmes are considered as "higher education" and not "VET" (Ministry of Education and Research, 2017[9]).

Work-based learning is required as part of VET programmes

Work-based learning, which includes both practical training in school workshops and experience with employers, is required in VET programmes, with specified percentage of minimum proportions of work-based learning in each programme – usually 50%, except for the upper secondary VET programmes that also include general education and therefore (in principle) give access to higher education, where the share is 35%. Within these totals, attention is given to the proportion of time spent with employers, as opposed to school workshops (Ministry of Education and Research, 2017[9]). This issue is further addressed in Chapter 2.

A small proportion of adult VET students pursue apprenticeships

Apprenticeships were established in 2006 as a specialised form of vocational education where the ratio of practical assignments undertaken in companies or institutions encompasses at least two-thirds of the curriculum. The student achieves the learning outcomes described in the curriculum by fulfilling working tasks at the company. The remainder of the studies will be undertaken at school. A contract between the school, student and employee is signed, setting out the rights and obligations of parties and the details of the learning programme. Wages are established at or above the statutory minimum wage established by the government. But it has proved very difficult to encourage employers to take on young apprentices, so the programme involves adults entirely (see Box 2.1 and the discussion in Chapter 2).

Russian language programmes are available in VET

Reforms currently in the course of implementation aim to deliver upper secondary education primarily in the Estonian language, but these reforms have proved slow to implement particularly in upper secondary VET schools. This may have led to an over-representation of Russian-speaking students in VET courses, but not because these students are interested in pursuing these programmes, but rather because they are in Russian.[3] To illustrate this point, 60% of boys who were in Russian language basic education in the north-eastern part of the country entered a VET programme at the upper secondary level, whereas only 10% of girls having studied in Estonian language in cities did so (Ministry of Education and Research, 2017[9]).

Assessment: Strengths, challenges and recommendations

Strengths

The context is favourable

Estonia has an exceptionally strong foundation and context for its VET system. The economy is strong, with high growth and relatively low unemployment. Both PISA and the Survey of Adults Skills, a product of the Programme for the International Assessment of Adult Competencies (PIAAC) results are very good by international standards, so that most young people have good basic skills, while even in the older generation, basic skills are relatively strong.

There is a strong system of occupational qualifications and examinations

Many countries have complex sets of overlapping and sometimes conflicting vocational qualifications. In Estonia, occupational qualification standards are defined and updated regularly with employer groups in sector skills councils. The standards are linked to a set of occupational examinations, which form the end point of different routes of preparation, including VET programmes, apprenticeships, and in some cases no formal programme, where the examinations are used to recognise prior learning, sometimes augmented by more informal preparatory courses. This provides a clear coherent foundation for the entire VET system, rooted in employer needs.

VET teachers are well-prepared

Countries often wrestle with the twin challenge of ensuring that on the one hand VET teachers are pedagogically effective, and on the other that they have relevant and up-to-date industry experience and knowledge. In Estonia, qualification requirements for VET teachers are less demanding than for teachers of general education subjects, allowing more flexibility for professionals who want to teach. There are three qualification levels for vocational teachers. To reach the highest level, the person should have at least EQF level 6 qualification in a tertiary vocational teacher programmes. Some vocational teachers work part time and have no pedagogical qualification, but a VET provider cannot employ more than 20% of staff with the lowest level qualification. Since 2015 professional development requirements for VET teachers have been made more flexible (CEDEFOP, 2017[15]).

VET schools and the school network have been overhauled

In the context of demographic change, much work has gone into an overhaul and consolidation of the VET school network. In 1990, there were over 90 VET schools. In 2016/17, 26 of 34 VET institutions were state-owned and run by the Ministry of Education and Research. Municipalities ran three VET schools and five were private. (A further five professional higher education institutions provided VET programmes at post-secondary level [ISCED 4] along with higher education [ISCED 6]). School facilities were extensively modernised between 2008 and 2015, using resources allocated by the European Regional Development Fund (Ministry of Education and Research, 2018[21]).

Employer-based learning is built into VET programmes

As discussed above, VET programmes in Estonia include minimum requirements for work-based learning, and these are augmented by expectations about the component of work-based learning that is genuinely employer-based. While more could be achieved in this area (see Chapter 2), this provides a good foundation of employer engagement for upper secondary vocational programmes.

Well-designed level 5 programmes have been developed

In some countries, because of the leading role of universities in post-secondary education, shorter vocational post-secondary programmes are squeezed out of the picture. In Estonia, for those who have completed upper secondary education, a relatively new EQF level 5 programme offers a post-secondary vocational programme in fields such as accountancy and business administration. Programmes last between six months and two and a half years, with work practice representing half of the course, divided equally between time with an employer and practice in the school environment. Nearly one-quarter of all VET learners are enrolled in these programmes (Ministry of Education and Research, 2017[9]).

An apprenticeship system has been introduced

Apprenticeship has proved its worth as an effective means of vocational education and training. As discussed above, in Estonia, apprenticeships, introduced in 2006, have gradually increased in number and they can now be pursued in multiple fields and at various qualification levels. While many challenges remain in further expanding apprenticeships and demonstrating their value for young people as well as adults, this represents a very promising initiative. This issue is further discussed in Chapter 2.

Recognition of prior learning is systematic

While many countries have recognised the potential of recognising prior learning (RPL), and many have systems in place, it is too often little used. In Estonia, general principles were set out in 2013 legislation, while the new lifelong learning strategy has further encouraged its development. Prior learning may be taken into account by education institutions when admitting learners to programmes and in exempting learners from a part of a curriculum. VET providers offering recognition of prior learning make public the terms that apply, and provide counselling to candidates. Multiple assessment techniques can be used to recognise prior learning (CEDEFOP, 2017[15]).

There is good provision for adults

Systematically, VET provision is designed not only to provide for the needs of young people after basic school, but also for adults at different stages in their life. VET programmes are therefore offered either in the form of an initial VET curriculum or in the form of continuous VET curriculum more suitable to adults, and often part-time study. The professional examinations can also be taken by adults, even if they have not pursued a formal programme of study (although this possibility might be developed further – see Chapter 3). As noted above, recognition of prior learning is widely available. Provision for adults is now underpinned by a new strategy on lifelong learning.

Career guidance is well-organised

Since 2009, the career counsellor network in the labour market sector has been co-ordinated by the public employment service. It offers career guidance services to the adult population. Since 2015, the service also provides workshops for young people in schools – students of grades 8 to 12 – to introduce them to the labour market and working life. These workshops are mostly financed from the EU budget. Career information specialists and counsellors work in every public employment service department. All guidance services for young people provided by *Rajaleidja* centres and the public employment service are free of charge. They are offered in individual and group settings, often accompanied by computer-based activities. There are professional standards for career counsellors, career information specialists and career co-ordinators at schools (Ministry of Education and Research, 2017[9]). Options for further developing career guidance in Estonia are set out in Chapter 4.

Challenges and recommendations

Many challenges remain

Despite these multiple achievements, there remain significant challenges in the VET system. Estonia now has a target of 35% of participation in upper secondary VET by 2020, increasing from the 26% of students who entered such programmes in 2016 (Ministry of Education and Research, 2017[9]). While this target of 35% is lower than some previous targets, it remains extremely demanding. Overall, modernisation of the VET system has not yet translated into an offer which graduates of basic education see as sufficiently attractive. Drop out rates have fallen, but remain too high for comfort. While apprenticeship has been launched, the development of youth apprenticeship, despite all its promise, has proved elusive. Upper secondary vocational programmes are still too often seen, and turn out to be, routes to the labour market, but not to further learning opportunities, including higher education. Perhaps reflecting wider factors in Estonia, the very large differences in career and education choices between women and men give cause for concern when placed alongside the evidence of a large gender pay gap by international standards. Again linked to wider factors, the position of the Russian-speaking minority, and language issues in the VET and other schools, raise significant challenges. While career guidance and counselling are well-developed in a formal sense, there are too few opportunities for young people in basic school to become familiar with the world of working life and different jobs.

The chapters that follow address these challenges

The three chapters that follow address these and other challenges, and advance policy recommendations. Here, those recommendations will simply be summarised, as follows:

Developing the foundations of the VET system (Chapter 2)

- Recommendation 2.1. Remove the risk of bias in the student's decision on whether to pursue general education or VET by continuing measures to separate upper secondary institutions from basic schools. Take advantage of local synergies to pursue collaboration between upper secondary general schools and VET schools, and merge general and VET schools where it is useful to do so.

- Recommendation 2.2. Tackle drop out by improving the financial incentives on schools to discourage drop out, and share wisdom on measures to encourage retention. To improve retention, and to support progression to higher level programmes, increase the attention given to the numeracy and literacy of students.
- Recommendation 2.3. Recognising its value, continue to develop work-based learning in enterprises as an essential part of the VET system. Building on existing quality assurance measures, set targets for employer-based work-based learning within VET programmes so that this element is formalised and made transparent through effective measurement. Explore options to overcome the barriers to youth apprenticeships.
- Recommendation 2.4. In the interests of equity, continue to monitor by gender/language spoken at home/region access and drop out. Use the evidence of monitoring to launch a policy development initiative to respond to disparities, developing appropriate responses through stakeholder consultation.

Pathways and progression (Chapter 3)

- Recommendation 3.1. Develop a multi-dimensional strategy to facilitate progression from initial VET. This strategy would recognise the need to work with different institutions and programmes across the education system, including career guidance within basic school as well as in VET institutions; building a dialogue with higher education institutions to establish the credentials of VET graduates as potential entrants to higher education; and addressing equity to ensure fair access to post-secondary and higher education by gender, region and mother tongue.
- Recommendation 3.2. Establish, within upper secondary VET, a hybrid programme to prepare students for the state examination offering access to higher education, as well as training them in their VET speciality. This approach would be designed to attract into VET more students with good school performance, and raise the status of VET in general.
- Recommendation 3.3. Building on the existing system of occupational examinations, further develop a higher-level examination system. This would follow the model of the dual system countries in providing higher level VET qualifications, particularly for working adults, for graduates of the initial VET system.
- Recommendation 3.4. Consider the option of a central fund, designed to target areas of specific skills shortage, and groups and regions with particular needs for reskilling, involving partnerships between employers and training providers, using the model of Swedish higher VET.

Strengthening career guidance (Chapter 4)

- Recommendation 4. Make some of the elements of the career guidance provision mandatory, in particular before grade 9, in all schools and in all classrooms, and monitor student participation to ensure that this goal is reached.
- Recommendation 4.2. Enhance use of data in career guidance, introducing destination surveys.
- Recommendation 4.3. Make sure that students get multiple opportunities to interact with people in work and workplaces.

Notes

[1] The Survey of Adult Skills (PIAAC) shows that 35% of Estonians are over-educated for their current jobs, and 17% are over-skilled (Flisi et al., 2016[22]).

[2] There is a state gymnasium reform going on – this means that there is going to be at least one high quality state-run gymnasium in each county by 2023 (there are 15 countries, the total number of institutions planned is 24). In the past, most of general upper secondary schools were owned by municipalities.

[3] Approximately one-third of year 9 in schools with Russian-speaking language of instruction do not reach the required B1 in Estonian at the end of basic education, which may point to ineffective teaching of Estonian in basic schools with Russian language of instruction.

References

Anspal, S. (2015), "Non-parametric decomposition and the choice of reference group: A study of the gender wage gap in 15 OECD countries", *International Journal of Manpower*, Vol. 36/8, pp. 1266-1280, https://doi.org/10.1108/IJM-03-2015. [8]

Anspa, S. and T. Rõõm (2007), *Gender Pay Gap in Estonia: Empirical Analysis*, https://www.sm.ee/sites/default/files/content-editors/Ministeerium_kontaktid/Valjaanded/gender_pay_gap_estonia_analysis.pdf. [6]

CEDEFOP (2017), *Vocational Education and Training in Estonia. Short Description*, Publications Office of the European Union, Luxembourg. [15]

Eesti Pank (2017), *Estonian Competitiveness Report*, Estonian Central Bank, Tallinn. [11]

Estonica (2018), "The impact of the enlightenment", http://www.estonica.org/en/Education_and_science/The_history_of_Estonian_education_%E2%80%94_the_story_of_the_intellectual_liberation_of_a_nation/The_impact_of_the_Enlightenment/ (accessed on 1 December 2018). [13]

EU Skills Panorama (2014), *Estonia Analytical Highlight*, ICT and Cedefop, https://skillspanorama.cedefop.europa.eu/en/analytical_highlights/prospects-estonia. [7]

Eurofound (2015), *Workers with Skills Matched to Their Duties*, European Working Conditions Survey, http://www.cedefop.europa.eu/en/publications-and-resources/statistics-and-indicators/statistics-and-graphs/27-what-extent-do-workers. [12]

Flisi, S. et al. (2016), "Measuring occupational mismatch: Overeducation and overskill in Europe - Evidence from PIAAC", *Social Indicators Research*, Vol. 131/3, pp. 1211-1249, http://dx.doi.org/10.1007/s11205-016-1292-7. [22]

Lees, M. (2016), *Estonian Education System 1990-2016 Reforms and their Impact*, Friedrich Naumann Foundation for Freedom, http://4liberty.eu/wp-content/uploads/2016/08/Estonian-Education-System_1990-2016.pdf. [14]

Ministry of Education and Research (2018), *PISA*, https://www.hm.ee/en/activities/statistics-and-analysis/pisa (accessed on 3 October 2018). [18]

Ministry of Education and Research (2018), *Vocational Education*, https://www.hm.ee/en/activities/vocational-education (accessed on 17 December 2018). [21]

Ministry of Education and Research (2017), *Background Report for OECD on Vocational Education and Training (VET) in Estonia*, http://www.hm.ee/sites/default/files/uuringud/oecd_vet_background.pdf. [9]

OECD (2018), "Population with tertiary education", *(indicator)*, http://dx.doi.org/10.1787/0b8f90e9-en (accessed on 28 September 2018). [16]

OECD (2018), "Unemployment rate", *(indicator)*, https://dx.doi.org/10.1787/997c8750-en (accessed on 5 October 2018). [4]

OECD (2017), *Building Skills for All in Australia: Policy Insights from the Survey of Adult Skills*, OECD Skills Studies, OECD Publishing, Paris, http://dx.doi.org/10.1787/9789264281110-en. [20]

OECD (2017), *OECD Economic Surveys: Estonia 2017*, OECD Publishing, Paris, http://dx.doi.org/10.1787/eco_surveys-est-2017-en. [3]

OECD (2016), *PISA 2015 Results (Volume I): Excellence and Equity in Education*, PISA, OECD Publishing, Paris, http://dx.doi.org/10.1787/9789264266490-en. [17]

OECD (2015), *OECD Economic Surveys: Estonia 2015*, OECD Publishing, Paris, http://dx.doi.org/10.1787/eco_surveys-est-2015-en. [5]

OECD (2015), *OECD Survey of Adult Skills (PIAAC) (Database 2012, 2015)*, http://www.oecd.org/skills/piaac/publicdataandanalysis/. [19]

OECD (2014), *Skills beyond School: Synthesis Report*, OECD Reviews of Vocational Education and Training, OECD Publishing, Paris, http://dx.doi.org/10.1787/9789264214682-en. [2]

OECD (2010), *Learning for Jobs*, OECD Reviews of Vocational Education and Training, OECD Publishing, Paris, http://dx.doi.org/10.1787/9789264087460-en. [1]

World Economic Forum (2016), *Global Competitiveness Report 2016-2017*, World Economic Forum, http://www3.weforum.org/docs/GCR2016-2017/05FullReport/TheGlobalCompetitivenessReport2016-2017_FINAL.pdf. [10]

Chapter 2. Developing the foundations of the vocational education and training system in Estonia

Only about one-quarter of the youth cohort enters vocational programmes at the upper secondary level, many of those with weak school attainment. Many students in Estonia attend full-cycle schools, which provide general education throughout the 12 grades, which biases the decision against vocational education and training (VET). While dropout rates have fallen, around one-quarter of entrants failing to complete. Apprentice numbers, although increasing, remain low and limited to adults. This chapter gives a set of recommendations that aim at removing the bias against VET and reducing dropout, while continuing to develop work-based learning. It also recommends better monitoring of VET participation by gender and student background.

Introduction

This chapter looks at the foundations of the vocational education and trainng system

Foundations mainly concerns the programmes in vocational schools, at upper secondary level, which young people enter in grade 10 – recognising that entrants to these programmes are also sometimes adults. Higher level post-secondary programmes, and transitions to higher education are addressed in Chapter 3.

Despite many strengths in the system, one challenge is low VET participation

As set out in Chapter 1, the strengths of the Estonian VET system, arising in large part from a sequence of recent reforms, are extensive. One of the challenges that remains arises partly because a relatively small part – about one-quarter – of the youth cohort enters VET, much less than in most European countries and less than comparable Nordic countries. In some strong vocational training systems, half or more of the youth cohort enter VET. Quite apart from the undoubted quality of vocational training systems, in Switzerland or Germany, there is an advantage in scale, because it means that the system naturally attracts some high ability students, who often go on into senior roles and become role models for young people considering whether to enter VET or general education. For example, in Switzerland, of top performers on the Programme for International Student Assessment (PISA), 25% enter the most demanding apprenticeship programmes leading to the professions of electronics engineer, commercial employee, optometrist and medical laboratory technicians[1] (Swiss Coordination Centre for Research in Education, 2014[1]). This helps to sustain a virtuous circle, in which young people want to enter vocational programmes because they aspire to follow these role models.

VET in Estonia tends to concentrate many students with weak school attainment

In Estonia, by contrast, VET tends, partly just because of its small scale, to concentrate those with the weakest basic skills and often special needs, and contains very few of the strongest performers. Dropout rates are worrying. Statistics on these points follow below. This means that a VET qualification may signal low ability to prospective employers, or to higher education institutions, handicapping a VET graduate even if they have received good quality training. Young people with ability and ambition will also be aware of this effect, and may therefore wish to avoid VET.

Achieving the target of 35% of young people entering VET would improve its status

Estonia's aspiration to increase the proportion of young people entering VET (to 35%) would in itself help to increase the status of VET. But, in a choice-driven system, increasing the proportion of young people who enter VET will depend on making VET more attractive, and that in its turn will depend on improved status for VET. This chapter therefore sets out some ideas about how to achieve that end.

Four main issues are addressed in this chapter, largely building on Estonia's existing direction of reform

First, consolidating existing reforms, the school network needs to ensure that the choice of VET or general education is not biased by a default option of remaining in the same full-cycle school. Second, reflecting Estonia's own target, action on drop out needs to build incentives for schools and teachers to tackle drop out, and to provide the tools to them to achieve this. Towards this end, basic skills gaps (literacy and numeracy) need to be addressed in a sustained way. Third, work-based learning needs to be further developed in schools through attention to workplace experience (and not just practical training). Apprenticeship, including the potential of youth apprenticeship, needs to be developed. Fourth, some equity issues need to be addressed, in terms of the variation, by gender, region and language spoken at home, in VET participation.

Characteristics of entrants and labour market outcomes

Entrants to VET tend to have weaker school results

The outcomes from upper secondary VET need to be assessed in relation to the characteristics of the student intake. In Estonia, of basic school graduates with very low-grade point averages (below 3.3), about 70% enter VET tracks (their choices on this point may be limited), while of those with top scores in GPA (above 4.6), only 2% opt for VET (Ministry of Education and Research, 2017[2]). In CEDEFOP's recent pan-European survey of attitudes towards VET, 70% of respondents in Estonia agreed that students with low grades are directed towards vocational education (CEDEFOP, 2017[3]). So although in Estonia the choice of a general or VET track is formally up to the student, the effects are highly selective, with most low-performing students strongly concentrated in the VET track.

Against that background the comparative earnings figures look good

Recent graduates with upper secondary VET qualifications earned slightly more than their counterparts with general upper secondary qualifications: for 2009 graduates, those with upper secondary vocational qualifications earned EUR 763 on average, those with general upper secondary qualifications EUR 705 on average (and those with basic education only earned just EUR 541 on average) (Jaggo, Reinhold and Valk, 2016[4]). There are a couple of elements here – the weakest students tend to drop out completely (40% of those with GPA's less than 3.29 drop out in the first year) and are therefore excluded from the analysis, while at the other end of the spectrum the best-performing students in general upper secondary education will go straight into higher education and will therefore also be excluded. That said, the figures still suggest that upper secondary VET is transitioning many young people into adequate, if not the best jobs.

But other research tells a more pessimistic story

While upper secondary VET, as noted above, seems to yield labour market outcomes similar and a bit better to general education, other sources show that its added value is not always very clear. The wages of upper secondary VET graduates are little different from wages of individuals with similar characteristics (age, gender and parental education) but with lower (below upper secondary) qualifications (Figure 2.1). The same analysis shows that, in some countries, VET yields a large wage premium. (CEDEFOP, 2013[5]), comparing outcomes in the labour market for graduates at ISCED 3 and 4 for 20-34 year-olds, found that in Estonia, although VET, relative to general education, increased the speed at which the first job after graduation is acquired, it also increased the risk that an individual was overqualified in their job. The risk of unemployment was not identifiably different between the two groups [see Table 21 in (CEDEFOP, 2013[5])]. One other indicator of outcomes is the risk of not being in education, training, or employment (NEET). In 2012, the OECD Survey of Adult Skills, a product of the Programme for the International Assessment of Adult Competencies (PIAAC) data showed that graduates from VET programmes were almost three times as likely to be NEET (21%), at the time of the survey, as graduates from general programmes (7%) (Figure 2.2).

Figure 2.1. In Estonia, limited evidence for a wage premium from VET among young adults

Percentage wage premia for graduates of upper secondary VET aged 16-40, relative to those with qualification levels below upper secondary, controlling for background characteristics

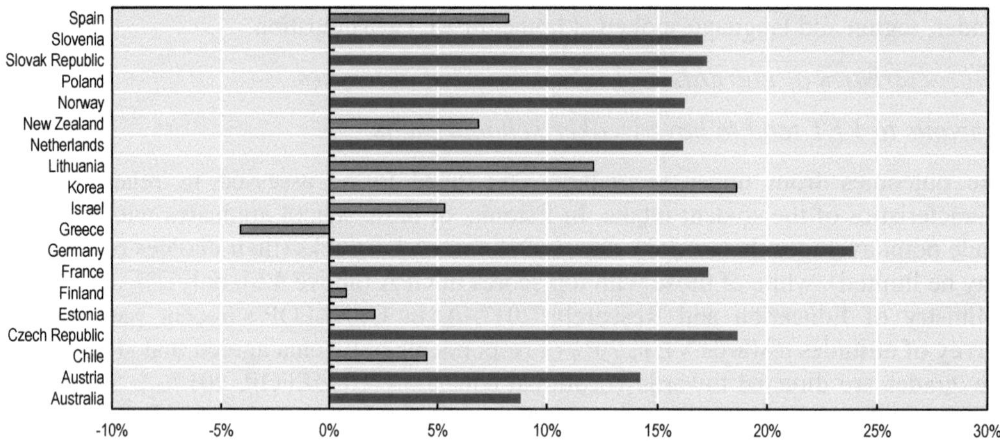

Note: Coefficients from the ordinary least squares (OLS) regression of log hourly earnings, adjusted for age, gender and parental education. Wage outliers above the 99th percentile and below the 1st percentile were dropped. Results that are statistically significant (at 5%) are in a darker tone. Lighter bars show premia too small for the difference from zero to be statistically significant. Those still in education are excluded from the analysis. Results are presented only for countries with a sufficient number of observations, and where VET can be distinguished from academic programmes.

Source: Calculations based on OECD (2015[6]), OECD Survey of Adult Skills (PIAAC) (Database 2012, 2015), www.oecd.org/skills/piaac/publicdataandanalysis/.

StatLink https://doi.org/10.1787/888933921738

Figure 2.2. VET graduates are more likely to be NEETs

Percentage of different upper secondary graduate groups (18-26) who are NEET, by programme orientation

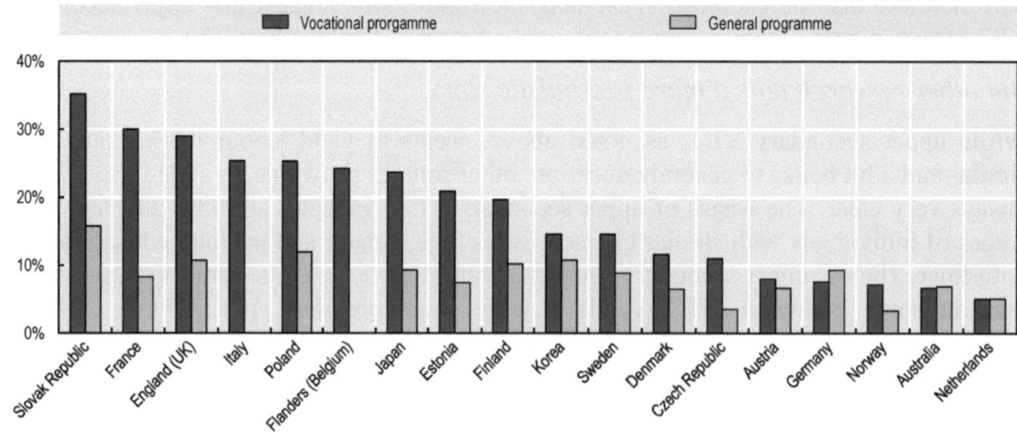

Note: Upper secondary VET includes programmes classified as ISCED 3C long, ISCED 3B and ISCED 3A identified by countries as vocationally oriented. For some countries results are not reported due to an insufficient number of observations.

Source: Calculations based OECD (2015[6]), OECD Survey of Adult Skills (PIAAC) (Database 2012, 2015), www.oecd.org/skills/piaac/publicdataandanalysis/.

StatLink https://doi.org/10.1787/888933921757

The main challenges

The structure of school institutions may bias students against the choice of VET

Full-cycle schools may bias students against VET

Many students in Estonia attend full-cycle schools, which provide general education throughout the 12 grades. There were 149 of these schools in 2017, compared with a few hundred basic schools offering grades below upper secondary (Ministry of Education and Research, 2017[2]). In full-cycle schools, young people in grade 9, at around the age of 15, face a choice about whether to remain in the same school and continue general education (although some students have to leave their basic education schools to enter academic gymnasiums), or alternatively, to move to a vocational school to pursue a vocational programme. Two factors may bias this decision against VET. One, suggested by some experts in Estonia (Ministry of Education and Research, 2017[2]), is that the guidance offered by the school, formally and informally, may be biased in favour of staying in the same school, either because of the school's direct financial interest (often in the context of demographic pressures on school rolls) or simply because teachers have an understandable bias in favour of their own institution and what it offers relative to alternative institutions. The other factor is that for students themselves at the age of 15, as they emerge into adulthood, friends and peer groups are extraordinarily important, and this will provide a powerful incentive for them to retain their friendship groups in their existing school. The net effect of all these factors is to powerfully bias choice away from vocational education in full-cycle schools.

Although there is no systematic selection between tracks, individual institutions can be selective

A decade ago, Darmody (2008[7]) described the process of competitive searching for a "good" upper secondary school place in Estonia. Although, formally, students can choose between general education and VET, in practice, some of the gymnasia, particularly in cities, tended to demand good grades and good behaviour. Only 12% of schools reported that they accepted all applicants. Geography also plays a big part in the selection process, as parents in rural areas sometimes have to send their children many kilometres to school. Dropout rates peak at grade 10, indicating the stresses of transition. Schools use entrance tests, but the admission requirements are school specific and there is no regulation over the admission rules (Põder and Lauri, 2014[8]). Overall and region-specific demographic changes substantially affect the scope for competition.

Drop out and challenges in basic skills

Dropout rates are worrying

Drop out has many costs to both individuals and society as a whole (Anspal et al., 2011[9]). Including those who change study area or school, around one out of five students drop out every year (19% in 2015/16). Around one-quarter of students drop out in their first year of VET, but many of them start again (Ministry of Education and Research, 2017[2]). Some drop out because they have found a job, or another study programme that suits them better, but only one out of ten of those who dropped out finish their vocational studies later on (Espenberg and al., 2012[10]). The end result is that in 2012, 21% of 20-28 year-olds have completed only basic education and lack upper secondary qualifications (Figure 2.3). This is a surprisingly high figure when set against the outstanding results achieved by many young Estonians in PISA for 15-year-olds. Such achievement should be, in principle, a solid foundation for continued upper secondary education; a number of countries - such as Canada, Germany and Poland - with worse PISA results, do better on this measure.

Table 2.1. Dropout rates in vocational programmes have fallen since 2013/14

Type of study	2011/12	2012/13	2013/14	2014/15	2015/16
EQF 2 and EQF 3 (including VET without basic education requirement)	39.3%	34.7%	38.3%	36.4%	24.9%
EQF 4 IVET ('upper-secondary VET')	17.7%	18.1%	19.4%	17.3%	16.1%
EQF 4 and EQF 5 (including post-secondary VET)	22.1%	22.2%	23.9%	22.7%	21.7%
Total	19.8%	20.2%	21.8%	20.3%	19.2%

Note: Drop outs exclude those who applied but never actually came to study, those who changed specialty in the same curriculum group (narrow field of study) in the same institution, or those who left and were readmitted within 31 days and continued studies in the same curriculum group. European Qualifications Framework (EQF).
Source: Adapted from Ministry of Education and Research (2017[2]), *Background Report for OECD on Vocational Education and Training (VET) in Estonia,*
www.hm.ee/sites/default/files/uuringud/oecd_vet_background.pdf

A reduction in dropout rates is part of Estonia's lifelong learning strategy

Dropout rates have been falling (Table 2.1) and as part of its lifelong learning strategy, Estonia has set a target to reduce dropout rates: the aim is to reduce the percentage of those aged 18-24 with at most lower secondary education and who are not in further education and training from 10.5% (the 2012 figure) to below 9% by 2020 (Ministry of Education and Research, 2014[11]).

Figure 2.3. In Estonia, one out of five young people have not completed upper secondary education

Percentage of 20-28 year-olds without an upper secondary qualification and who are not currently in education, 2012

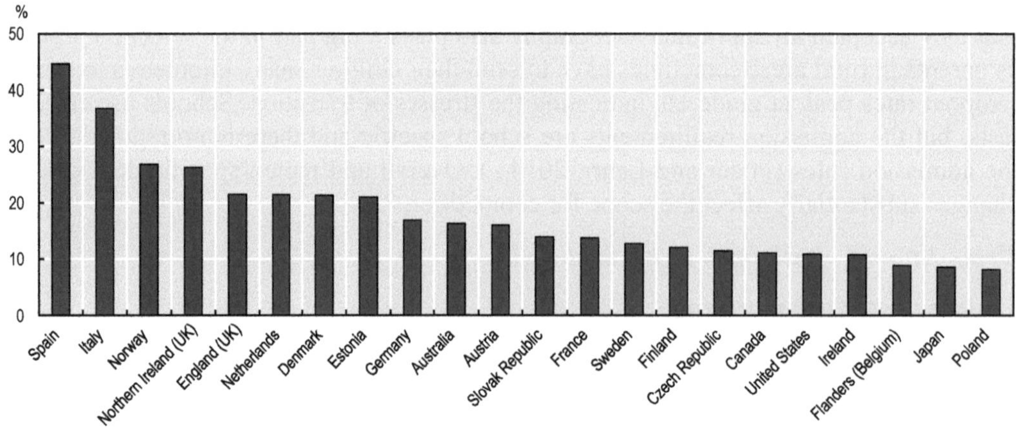

Note: Adults with foreign qualifications and 1st generation migrants who obtained their highest qualification prior to entering the country are excluded. For some countries results are not reported due to insufficient number of observations.
Source: Calculations based on OECD (2015[6]), OECD Survey of Adult Skills (PIAAC) (Database 2012, 2015), www.oecd.org/site/piaac/publicdataandanalysis.htm.

StatLink https://doi.org/10.1787/888933921776

The incentives on teachers and school leaders to prevent drop out are mixed at best

One often unspoken challenge is that the incentives on schools to prevent drop out are often lacking. Students at risk of dropping out are often demotivated, and may struggle with their classwork, or, because of other problems or stresses on their lives, display behavioural difficulties. These students will therefore usually present the greatest teaching challenges, and if they do not appear at the school, the immediate effect will be to ease the pressure on teachers. Of course, most teachers and school leaders recognise that it is their professional responsibility to seek to engage those at risk, and prevent drop out, but there are few rewards for them or their institutions from doing so.

There are no funding incentives encouraging VET schools to tackle drop out

Funding levels in VET are set by the State Commission for Vocational Education. The commission decides on priority programmes, what they should cost, and how many students should be enrolled in them. The numbers of funded study places in each school and each programme in individual VET schools is determined for a three-year planning period, following consultation between government, industry and the schools. This schools funding arrangement remains in place, even if the planned number of students is not recruited, regardless of drop out. So drop out has no direct financial cost to a school (Santiago et al., 2016[12]). This arrangement is apparently now under review, with the government integrating some amount of performance funding (dependant on completion rates).

Table 2.2. VET graduates have lower numeracy and literacy skills than general education programmes' graduates

Numeracy performance in score points of those aged 16-34 with upper secondary as highest qualification, (standard errors in brackets)

	Numeracy			Literacy		
	Academic	VET	Difference	Academic	VET	Difference
Australia	279 (3)	266 (3)	13	294 (3)	274 (3)	20
Austria	311 (4)	274 (2)	37	307(3)	272 (2)	35
Denmark	299 (3)	278 (3)	21	300 (2)	269 (3)	31
Estonia	294 (2)	264 (3)	30	297 (2)	269 (3)	28
Finland	311 (2)	280 (2)	31	319 (2)	290(2)	29
France	285 (2)	248 (2)	37	295 (2)	260 (2)	35
Germany	306 (3)	268 (3)	38	308 (2)	267 (3)	41
Norway	293 (3)	276 (3)	17	319 (2)	286 (2)	33
Netherlands	314 (2)	279 (2)	35	294 (2)	275 (3)	19
Spain	270 (2)	254 (7)	16	278 (2)	258 (5)	20
Sweden	297 (3)	281 (3)	16	299 (2)	281 (3)	18

Note: Adults who obtained their highest qualification outside the country, those with foreign qualifications and 1st generation migrants who obtained their highest qualification prior to entering the host country are excluded.
Source: Calculations based on OECD (2015[6]), OECD Survey of Adult Skills (PIAAC) (Database 2012, 2015), www.oecd.org/site/piaac/publicdataandanalysis.htm.

There is strong evidence that weak basic skills are a cause of drop out

One potential cause of drop out is weak basic skills, in link also to weak school attainment. Of those with a grade point score on graduation from basic school of under

3.3, nearly 40% drop out in the first year of upper secondary VET studies, compared with only 9% of their counterparts with scores of at least 4.3. As in other countries, those aged 16-34 with upper secondary vocational education as their highest qualification have weaker basic skills than those with general academic upper secondary qualifications[2] (Table 2.2). Of those who have not completed upper secondary school, 34% have low numeracy skills, compared to 13% of those who have completed upper secondary education (Figure 2.4).

Figure 2.4. Some early school leavers lack numeracy skills

Percentage scoring below level 2 in numeracy among (a) those aged 20-28 without upper secondary education, (b) those whose highest qualification is at upper secondary level

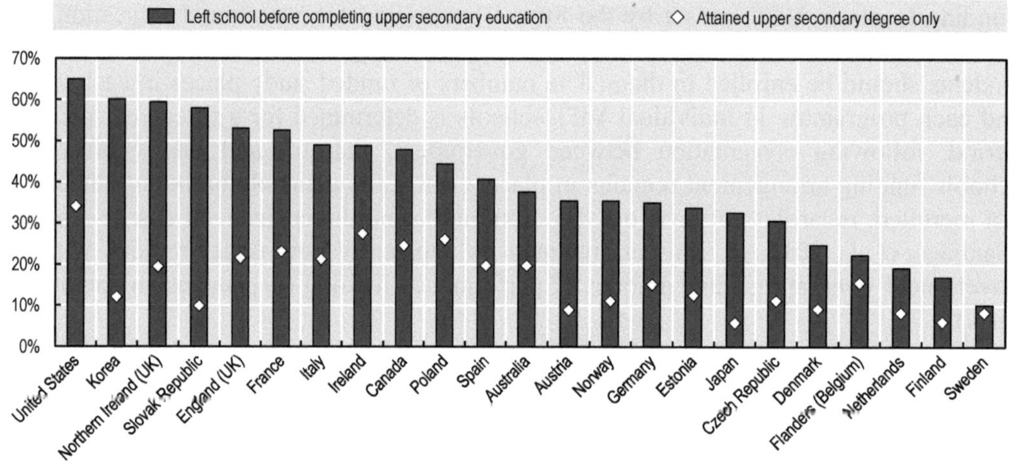

Note: Adults with foreign qualifications and 1st generation migrants who obtained their highest qualification prior to entering the country are excluded, 16-65 year olds.
Source: Calculations based on OECD (2015[6]), OECD Survey of Adult Skills (PIAAC) (Database 2012, 2015), www.oecd.org/site/piaac/publicdataandanalysis.htm.

StatLink ᐧᒥᔅᑭ https://doi.org/10.1787/888933921795

Work-based learning and apprenticeships

While work-based learning is required, it does not necessarily include experience with employers

For VET programmes leading to EQF 3, 4 and 5, work-based learning (WBL) is expected to be at least 50% of the programme (Ministry of Education and Research, 2017[2]). However, WBL is defined as including both work practice at enterprises, and practical workshops in school. There is evidence that there is a particular value on experience in actual workplaces, because of the potential for learning multiple soft skills (such as dealing with customers) and because of the value of contact with employers. (Chankseliani, Keep and Wilde, 2017[13]), for example, describe the diverse literature which emphasises the value of learning through demanding, difficult work, and how this can engage and empower the learner in ways that cannot be replicated by off-the-job training.

In Estonia, the OECD team were told that the proportion of actual work practice in enterprises within "work-based learning" is monitored by the Ministry of Education and Research, and through the quality assurance regime, so that individual vocational schools would not be permitted to run programmes offering minimal or zero actual workplace experience to students.

Apprenticeship is currently a small-scale programme for adults

At present, apprenticeship is very small in scale in Estonia with around 1 300 places in 2017. Since 2007, in principle VET programmes (that can lead to EQF levels 2-5) can be offered as apprenticeships, with at least two-thirds of the programme taking place in the enterprise. The principles of the apprenticeship system design are consistent with many international models (Box 2.1). While the programme is intended to be applicable both to incumbent workers needing to upskill or reskill, and new recruits, in practice the programme has been dominated by adult incumbent workers, with an average age of 38 for apprentices. It has not proved possible to interest employers in taking youth apprentices. Given the success of youth apprenticeship in some other countries, this must be a concern.

Box 2.1. Apprenticeship in Estonia

In an Estonian apprenticeship, the school, the enterprise and the apprentice sign a contract (*praktikaleping*), where the duties and responsibilities of each party are outlined. An individualised curriculum specifying the learning outcomes is attached to the contract. One-third of the curriculum is delivered at a VET institution with an emphasis on theoretical training, and two-thirds at an enterprise; the apprentice has two appointed supervisors, one at the school and another at the workplace. Apprentices receive a wage during the training at the enterprise and a study allowance during studies at school. Unless the apprentice already has a work contract, the wage is agreed upon in the tripartite contract and it cannot be lower than the minimum salary set by the government. Studies are complete after passing a professional or vocational examination. The apprenticeship is in most (but not all) cases launched on the initiative of the school, and the school co-ordinates the development of a curriculum and the admission process of apprentices.

An apprenticeship programme is usually funded through the State-commissioned study places scheme. The school covers the training at school, supervisors' training and salary for the school supervisor. The school can transfer up to 50% of the cost of the study place to the enterprise to cover the salary cost of workplace supervisors.

In 2017 there were about 1 300 apprentices, up from 700 the previous year. With funding from the European Social Fund, it is intended to create 8 000 additional places by 2020. Development activities will focus on training and co-operation between supervisors at schools and at enterprises, best practices will be shared, and the best enterprises will be acknowledged. Resources will be created on how to implement work-place learning and pilots will be run. By the end of 2016, 185 work practice (internship) supervisors and supervisors in apprenticeship training had received continuing professional development (CPD) training.

Source: Ministry of Education and Research, (2017[2]), *Background Report for OECD on Vocational Education and Training (VET) in Estonia*, www.hm.ee/sites/default/files/uuringud/oecd_vet_background.pdf.

Large variations in VET participation, by gender and language and region

VET systems are expected to serve both aspiration and inclusion

All countries face competing pressures on their VET systems. On the one hand, as discussed here in the context of Estonia, many countries are seeking to raise the status of their VET systems so that VET is, and is seen to be, of high status and high quality: an option that can be a good choice for higher achieving young people, including those with aspirations to continue their studies in higher education. At the same time, in Estonia, as in many other countries, a large proportion of those young people who face the greatest challenges in their school attainment choose, or are selected into, vocational programmes. VET therefore has to serve a very important equity function, integrating and supporting many of the young students facing the greatest challenges. Meeting both of these challenges at the same time, so that VET is a vehicle for both aspiration and inclusion, creates significant policy dilemmas, particularly when it comes to deciding how demanding the VET programmes should be.

Some large disparities in VET participation exist between different demographic groups

Many of the broader challenges of inclusion are addressed here under the heading of drop out. But there are also equity challenges faced by particular groups. Only 10% of girls who graduate in bigger cities, having studied in Estonian, choose VET, whereas in North-East Estonia, 60% of boys with Russian as the instruction language, opt for VET. Of learners who have not achieved B1 in Estonian by the end of basic school (presumably mostly those with Russian mother tongue), two-thirds have continued in VET (Ministry of Education and Research, 2017[2]). The OECD team were told that monitoring of these potential equity issues is quite systematic, but did not necessarily lead to any firm diagnosis of action.

Recommendations

To address the challenges described, the following recommendations are advanced:

- Recommendation 2.1. Remove the risk of bias in the student's decision on whether to pursue general education or VET by continuing measures to separate upper secondary institutions from basic schools. Take advantage of local synergies to pursue collaboration between upper secondary general schools and VET schools, and merge general and VET schools where it is useful to do so.

- Recommendation 2.2. Tackle drop out by improving the financial incentives on schools to discourage drop out, and share wisdom on measures to encourage retention. To improve retention, and to support progression to higher level programmes, increase the attention given to the numeracy and literacy of students.

- Recommendation 2.3. Recognising its value, continue to develop work-based learning in enterprises as an essential part of the VET system. Building on existing quality assurance measures, set targets for employer-based work-based learning within VET programmes so that this element is formalised and made transparent through effective measurement. Explore options to overcome the barriers to youth apprenticeships.

- Recommendation 2.4. In the interests of equity, continue to monitor by gender/language spoken at home/region access and drop out. Use the evidence of monitoring to launch a policy development initiative to respond to disparities, developing appropriate responses through stakeholder consultation.

Analysis and supporting arguments

Develop the school network so as to eliminate potential bias in the choice between VET and general education.

Recommendation 2.1. Remove the risk of bias in the student's decision on whether to pursue general education or VET by continuing measures to separate upper secondary institutions from basic schools. Take advantage of local synergies to pursue collaboration between upper secondary general schools and VET schools, and merge general and VET schools where it is useful to do so.

On this issue, the government is pursuing some welcome action

The Ministry of Education and Research had, by 2017, founded about a dozen new state-run upper secondary schools in different regions, with plans to reach 24 by 2023. The ministry intends this reform to develop stronger co-operation between these general education institutions and VET schools, to reduce barriers between different types of school and ensure more efficient use of resources (Ministry of Education and Research, 2017[2]).

This process is welcome, but needs to go further

One option would be for the ministry to take over responsibility for grades 10-12 within existing full-cycle schools, and establishing a clear break point at grade 9. In the first instance, this might involve establishing a divide within existing schools, but over time, a separation would develop, given separate governance arrangements, with both vocational and general upper secondary education at grades 10-12 managed mainly by central government, while basic schools in grades 1-9 would be managed by municipalities. This separation would help to establish grade 9 as a point where students decide on their choice of VET or general track, without any default option of simply staying in the same school.

Collaboration and in some cases mergers, between general and VET schools should be encouraged

The common governance arrangements for general and VET schools at grades 9-12 would and should also help to reinforce links between the two types of school, and in some cases mergers. Closer links would preserve the strategic objective of permeability between the two pathways and allow the sharing of equipment and infrastructure. This would build on some existing good Estonian experience, including:

- VET institutions provide optional vocational courses (i.e. in the fields of information and communication technology [ICT], car technician, facility services, woodworking, music) to the learners of basic school or general upper-secondary school (Ministry of Education and Research, 2017[2]).
- Three state-owned institutions (one general upper-secondary school, two VET institutions) in the county of Viljandi arranged a joint campaign for basic school graduates to introduce learning opportunities at the upper-secondary level (Ministry of Education and Research, 2017[2]).

This parallels initiatives in other countries

Norway and Sweden maintain some integrated, VET and general education upper secondary schools. Other types of measures such as increasing the number of general subject courses within vocational programmes (this has been the case in Norway), or to offer students a menu of options drawn from both general education and vocational programmes. Sweden has modularised vocational programmes, such that students enrolled in upper secondary VET can transfer completed courses to any other programme at the upper secondary level, including general education (Skolverket and ReferNet Sweden, 2016[14]).

Tackle drop out and address the basic skills of students

Recommendation 2.2. Tackle drop out by improving the financial incentives on schools to discourage drop out, and share wisdom on measures to encourage retention. To improve retention, and to support progression to higher level programmes, give attention to the numeracy and literacy of students.

Funding arrangements should provide financial incentives for schools to retain students

To address drop out, the first priority is to provide incentives on VET institutions to reduce drop out. As argued in the OECD's review of school resources in Estonia (Santiago et al., 2016[12]), and in line with plans already under way in Estonia to introduce performance-based funding, Estonia should introduce, for VET institutions, an element of student per capita funding associated with retention and completion. This might, for example link funding for schools to head counts of students who are attending VET programmes (rather than, as at present, just to planned numbers of students in particular fields of study). This would incentivise recruitment and retention. One element of the per capita funding might also be associated with a measure of completion. Such measures would need to be handled carefully to avoid the risk of institutions "gaming" the funding regime, for example by avoiding the admission of students who are at risk of drop out, or in other ways (Santiago et al., 2016[12]).

As well as incentives, VET institutions need the tools to tackle drop out

There are a myriad of initiatives in different countries, and often multiple tools are helpful, bearing in mind that quite diverse factors may be responsible for drop out in individual cases. Some European experience is summarised in the report of the RESL.EU exercise (RESL.EU, 2013[15]). There is also extensive experience in the United States: the National Dropout Prevention Center proposes 15 strategies to prevent drop out, including, for example, personalised learning strategies, family engagement, after-school and out-of-school opportunities, mentoring and tutoring, professional development for the staff most involved in dropout prevention, and school-community collaboration, among other strategies (National Dropout Prevention Center, 2018[16]). The foundation of any approach to drop out is a mechanism to identify those at risk, so that interventions can be targeted on them, and an individualised approach, recognising that the causes of drop out are diverse. Strong career guidance, ensuring that students are fully understand the programmes of study which they pursue in the light of career aspirations which have been developed in the context of professional counselling, is also associated with lower levels of drop out. Career guidance is discussed in Chapter 4 of this report.

Increased attention to literacy and numeracy can help to tackle drop out

As described above, weak basic skills are closely correlated with drop out, strongly suggesting that weak basic skills are a cause of drop out, most plausibly because numeracy and literacy are foundational skills, underpinning the capacity to learn other types of knowledge and skills. This means that one very promising way of tackling drop out might be to undertake targeted efforts to tackle weak numeracy and literacy. As an indicator of the potential, one study in England (United Kingdom) showed that, of a group of further education students identified as needing remedial basic skills support, those that went on to receive that support were fully three times less likely to drop out than those who did not receive such support (Basic Skills Agency, 1997[17]). (While the group who opted to receive support in this study were probably more motivated, the size of the difference strongly suggests that basic skills support promoted successful completion).

Box 2.2. The I-BEST programme, Washington State in the United States

The I-BEST programme combines basic skills teaching and professional training, typically in a classroom setting in which there is both a basic skills educator and a professional trainer. The professional training, offered in fields of skills shortage, yields college credits and contributes to a certificate credential. I-BEST programmes are available in every community and technical college. Individuals must score below a certain threshold on an adult skill test and qualify for adult basic education to participate in an I-BEST programme. In practice, this translates to around 2% of basic skills students.

Studies measuring the impact of I-BEST in Washington State found that I-BEST students earn more credits and are more likely to complete a programme than a comparable group of students not participating in the programme. Evidence on the link between participation in I-BEST and earnings is less conclusive, although this might be due to changing economic conditions.

Source: Kuczera, M. and S. Field (2013[18]), *A Skills beyond School Review of the United States*, OECD Reviews of Vocational Education and Training, http://dx.doi.org/10.1787/9789264202153-en.

Sometimes contextual learning may help students in vocational programmes to acquire basic skills

Some care needs to be taken with remedial basic skills education. For those who have struggled with mathematics through basic school, extra maths classes in grades 10-12 vocational programmes may be demotivating or ineffective, and could simply precipitate drop out. One alternative is contextual learning, in which numeracy and literacy skills are conveyed in the context of other learning programmes. Contextual learning is theoretically convincing, and there have been successful programmes, but it can be demanding of teachers and is usually resource-intensive. The I-BEST model in the United States is one promising initiative of this type (Box 2.2). In Norway, the Transition Project identifies the lowest performing students at the end of school year 10 and in upper secondary education and provides them with additional support in core skills. The project works with teachers to provide concrete strategies for making Norwegian, English and mathematics more meaningful to students' lives. It also instructs teachers on ways to provide basic remediation to struggling students when this may not have been the focus in secondary teachers' pre-service preparation (OECD, 2012[19]).

But there are other strong reasons to encouraging strong basic skills in vocational programmes

The prevention of drop out is only one of many reasons for emphasising numeracy and literacy in vocational programmes. These foundational skills underpin further learning and the capacity to adapt, both in work, and in the context of further and higher education (Heckman, 2008[20]). Pathways of progression are vital if VET is not to be a dead end – issues which are considered in depth in Chapter 3. This also means that basic skills should not just be seen as a remedial exercise for those with particular weaknesses, but also as a foundation for further learning which will be essential for those who aspire to continue to higher education and other post-secondary programmes. Strong literacy and numeracy skills are also associated with entrepreneurship and success in business activities, and with a lowered risk of poverty (World Bank, 2012[21]).

Continue efforts to develop work-based learning

> *Recommendation 2.3. Recognising its value, continue to develop work-based learning in enterprises as an essential part of the VET system. Building on existing quality assurance measures, set targets for employer-based work-based learning within VET programmes so that this element is formalised and made transparent through effective measurement. Explore options to overcome the barriers to youth apprenticeships.*

Special attention should be given to work practice with employers in VET programmes

There are grounds for giving special attention to work practice in enterprises, as opposed to school workshop training, in the context of Estonia's definition of work-based learning, which includes both. While this is already recognised in Estonia in practice through the regulatory role of the ministry and through quality assurance, it is an important issue which deserves to be formalised. In the first instance, data should be systematically collected on the extent of workplace experience in VET programmes. This might then provide a basis for setting a minimum expectation on the required amount of workplace experience. For example, in Sweden, students enrolled on three-year upper secondary vocational provision must spend at least fifteen weeks applying their skills in workplaces. In the Netherlands, school-based VET includes the requirement that all students pursue at least 20% of their time in work placements with employers (i.e. not just in school workshops) (Fazekas and Litjens, 2014[22]). One advantage of this model is that the availability of work placements then provides a means of guiding the mix of provision in VET towards the needs of the labour market. In the Netherlands, for example, data are collected on the relative difficulty of finding work placements in different fields, and those entering VET are warned off fields which, although sometimes popular with students, offer few work placements. This may be upsetting for the students at the time, but it is better to find out that employers have little interest in recruiting individuals in a particular field of study before, rather than after, training in that field.

Evidence shows that apprenticeships smooth transition to the labour market

There are also grounds for pursuing efforts to encourage youth apprenticeships. While initial attempts to launch youth apprenticeship in Estonia have not been successful, because employers are apparently reluctant to participate, the potential advantages of youth apprenticeship are so strong that continued efforts are justified. In summary, the evidence shows that apprenticeships smooth transitions to work (Nilsen and Bratberg, 2000[23]; Samek et al., 2013[24]; Kuczera, 2017[25]). Overall, countries with a high share of young people in apprenticeships have lower rates of disconnected youth and youth experiencing a difficult transition to employment (Quintini and Manfredi, 2009[26]).[3] Apprenticeships help to engage disconnected youth as they offer an opportunity to learn and connect to the world of work through a form of learning that might be more appealing than more academic programmes (CEDEFOP, 2017[3]; Kis, 2016[27]).

But to expand, they need to meet the needs of young people better

Some apprenticeship systems serve primarily to transition young people from school to work. In Switzerland for example, in 2014/15, three-quarters (76%) of apprentices were under 20. But other countries have a more even mix of adult and youth apprentices, with some of the adults already having significant work experience. In Germany in 2014, around 56% of apprentices were under 20, and a further 20% were between 21 and 23-years-old, the older apprentices being a mix of those who complete the academic upper secondary *Abitur* before entering apprenticeship, and others who have often spent some time in pre-apprenticeship programmes (Mühlemann, 2016[28]). In 2010 and 2011, 20-year-olds and older represented more than 50% of all apprentices in Finland (Stenström and Virolainen, 2014[29]).

Estonia's tight labour market should facilitate youth apprenticeship

In Estonia, low unemployment rates and skills shortages in at least some areas should, in principle, provide fertile ground to encourage youth apprenticeship. For employers, there is a learning curve with apprenticeship. Some employers are already becoming familiar with adult apprenticeships and how they work. One might start small, and encourage youth apprenticeship in a particular industry or region where circumstances are most favourable. It would also be worthwhile considering the offer of a special incentive to employers to take young apprentices. Employers who do so are in effect providing part of the school to work infrastructure which benefits everyone. Some other countries, such as Korea and Norway, provide employers with financial incentives. While the evidence is that these incentives have a limited impact, symbolically they may be important, and might help to launch youth apprenticeship in Estonia.

The wage paid to apprentices might be too high in Estonia to encourage the development of apprenticeships for young people

In some countries, apprentice wages commonly increase gradually but substantially over the period of the apprenticeship, reflecting increasing skills and productivity (Kuczera, 2017[25]). In Estonia, there is a requirement to pay the minimum wage to apprentices, but only the work placement bit of the training programmes[4] (Ministry of Education and Research, 2017[2]). Estonia might consider the implementation of an apprentice wage, lower than the minimum wage, to convince employers to take on younger apprentices.

Monitor and respond to variations in VET participation

Recommendation 2.4. In the interests of equity, continue to monitor by gender/language spoken at home/region access and drop out. Use the evidence of monitoring to launch a policy development initiative to respond to disparities, developing appropriate responses through stakeholder consultation.

Large differences in participation rates need to be investigated

While it would not be reasonable to expect that every demographic group would or should display exactly the same propensity to pursue VET programmes, some of the large disparities which can be observed in Estonia suggest that some other factors may be at work, and these could be limiting or narrowing career aspirations or expectations. One year after graduation from basic school, 38% of students opting for Russian-speaking instruction were in VET tracks, compared with just 25% of those opting for Estonian-speaking instruction (Santiago et al., 2016[12]).

The policy objective is to ensure that young people from all demographic groups have similar opportunities to realise their potential

The objective of policy in this area is to ensure that all individuals should have the fullest opportunity to achieve their potential, and that different demographic groups defined by language spoken at home, gender or region should have the same opportunities. Sometimes, raw disparities in participation rates may signal that this is not happening. The policy response needs to be modulated. For example, for girls graduating from basic schools in Tallinn and other large cities, it may not be in the best interests of all 90% of them to enter general education, recognising that some of them with weaker academic performance may find it very difficult to enter higher education, and a general upper secondary education may not equip them as effectively for the labour market as a vocational programme would do. One response might be more active and effective guidance targeted at this group. Some of it may need to address gender stereotypes in target professions. This point is further discussed in Chapter 4.

A key test is whether, if any group is over-represented in VET, that provides them with good opportunities for careers and further learning

Similarly, in the North East of the country, 60% of Russian speakers choose VET tracks. It would be helpful to know their labour market outcomes. One response to this finding might be to further explore the extent to which this group progresses into further and higher education. If they do so, then the VET track may not be inhibiting their career prospects. If 70% of any demographic group choose VET, it would be reasonable to expect a proportion of them to be able to benefit from further and higher education. Many of the observed variations in participation between demographic groups certainly reflect attitudes and aspirations that have developed over long periods.

The policy response to observed differences needs to be developed carefully

While monitoring already takes place extensively, the OECD team were told that policy responses are limited. This is challenging territory, since observed disparities in education participation often reflect a complex mix of choice and constraint. Often the policy response will need to be multi-faceted, so as to change career expectations and stereotypes. With this in mind Estonia should consider launching a funded initiative to address the equity issues in VET, and to explore with multiple stakeholders some potential solutions. There is scope to explore experimental initiatives in individual schools and regions to address equity challenges.

Notes

[1] It should be noted that in some countries some of the occupations listed here require enrolling in a university programme.

[2] Of course comparison of scores from the Survey of Adult Skills (PIAAC) between track orientation need to take into account that those in pre-vocational tracks at age 15 have much weaker performance in maths and literacy than their peers in general tracks, as shown in PISA.

[3] Quintini and Manfredi (2009[26]) show that in countries with regulated labour markets and strong apprenticeship systems, such as Germany, about 80% of school leavers succeed in integrating into the labour market, a marked contrast to countries without strong work-based training such as Italy and Spain. However, this advantage fades over time, as participants in other types of education establish a foothold in the labour market.

[4] Apprentices receive a wage during the training at the enterprise and a study allowance during studies at school. Unless the apprentice already has a work contract, the wage is agreed upon in the tripartite contract and it cannot be lower than the minimum salary set by the government. The minimum monthly gross salary in 2017 is EUR 470, (full-time work), the average monthly gross salary in 2016 was EUR 1 146 (Ministry of Education and Research, 2017[2]).

References

Anspal, S. et al. (2011), *Õpingute ebaõnnestumise kulud Eestis*, (The cost of unsuccessful studies in Estonia), CentAR, Tallinn. [9]

Basic Skills Agency (1997), *Staying the Course. The Relationship between Basic Skills Support, Drop Out, Retention and Achievement in Further Education Colleges*, Basic Skills Agency, London. [17]

CEDEFOP (2017), *Cedefop European Public Opinion Survey on Vocational Education and Training*, Publications Office of the European Union, Luxembourg. [3]

CEDEFOP (2013), "Labour market outcomes of vocational education in Europe. Evidence from the European Union labour force survey", *Research Paper*, No. 32, Publications Office of the European Union, Luxembourg, http://www.cedefop.europa.eu/files/5532_en.pdf. [5]

Chankseliani, M., E. Keep and S. Wilde (2017), *People and Policy: A Comparative Study of Apprenticeship Across Eight National Contexts*, WISE, University of Oxford. [13]

Darmody, M. (2008), "Transition to upper secondary school: an Estonian experience", *Journal of Baltic Studies*, Vol. 39/2, pp. 185-208. [7]

Espenberg, K. and E. al. (2012), *Õpingute Katkestamise Põhjused Kutseõppes*, (Reasons for Discontinuing Attendance of Vocational Education), University of Tartu Applied Social Sciences Research Centre (RAKE) and CPD OÜ, Tartu, https://www.hm.ee/sites/default/files/opingute_katkestamise_pohjused_kutseoppes.pdf. [10]

Fazekas, M. and I. Litjens (2014), *A Skills beyond School Review of the Netherlands*, OECD
Reviews of Vocational Education and Training, OECD Publishing, Paris,
http://dx.doi.org/10.1787/9789264221840-en.   [22]

Heckman, J. (2008), "Schools, skills, and synapses", *Economic Inquiry*, Vol. 46/3, pp. 289-324,
http://dx.doi.org/10.1111/j.1465-7295.2008.00163.x.   [20]

Jaggo, I., M. Reinhold and A. Valk (2016), *Labour Market Success of Vocational and Higher
Education*, Analysis Department of the Ministry of Education and Research.   [4]

Kis, V. (2016), "Work-based learning for youth at risk: Getting employers on board", *OECD
Education Working Papers*, No. 150, OECD Publishing, Paris,
https://dx.doi.org/10.1787/5e122a91-en.   [27]

Kuczera, M. (2017), "Striking the right balance: Costs and benefits of apprenticeship", *OECD
Education Working Papers*, No. 153, OECD Publishing, Paris,
http://dx.doi.org/10.1787/995fff01-en.   [25]

Kuczera, M. and S. Field (2013), *A Skills beyond School Review of the United States*, OECD
Reviews of Vocational Education and Training, OECD Publishing, Paris,
http://dx.doi.org/10.1787/9789264202153-en.   [18]

Ministry of Education and Research (2017), *Background Report for OECD on Vocational
Education and Training (VET) in Estonia*,
http://www.hm.ee/sites/default/files/uuringud/oecd_vet_background.pdf.   [2]

Ministry of Education and Research (2014), *The Estonian Lifelong Learning Strategy 2020*,
https://www.hm.ee/sites/default/files/estonian_lifelong_strategy.pdf.   [11]

Mühlemann, S. (2016), "The cost and benefits of work-based learning", *OECD Education
Working Papers*, No. 143, OECD Publishing, Paris, http://dx.doi.org/10.1787/5jlpl4s6g0zv-
en.   [28]

National Dropout Prevention Center (2018), *National Prevention Centre*,
http://www.dropoutprevention.org (accessed on 12 June 2018).   [16]

Nilsen, Ø. and E. Bratberg (2000), "Transitions from school to work: Search time and job
duration", *IZA Discussion Paper*, Vol. 27, https://ssrn.com/abstract=166560.   [23]

OECD (2015), *OECD Survey of Adult Skills (PIAAC) (Database 2012, 2015)*,
http://www.oecd.org/skills/piaac/publicdataandanalysis/.   [6]

OECD (2012), *Equity and Quality in Education: Supporting Disadvantaged Students and
Schools*, OECD Publishing, Paris, http://dx.doi.org/10.1787/9789264130852-en.   [19]

Põder, K. and T. Lauri (2014), "Will choice hurt? Compared to what? A school choice
experiment in Estonia", *Journal of School Choice*, Vol. 8/3, pp. 446-474,
http://dx.doi.org/10.1080/15582159.2014.942177.   [8]

Quintini, G. and T. Manfredi (2009), "Going separate ways? School-to-work transitions in the United States and Europe", *OECD Social, Employment and Migration Working Papers*, No. 90, OECD Publishing, Paris, http://dx.doi.org/10.1787/221717700447. [26]

RESL.EU (2013), *Policies on Early School Leaving in Nine European Countries: A Comparative Perspective*, RESL.eu project, http://ec.europa.eu/research/social-sciences/pdf/policies_early_school_leaving.pdf. [15]

Samek, M. et al. (2013), *The Effectiveness and Costs-Benefits of Apprenticeships: Results of the Quantitative Analysis*, European Commission. [24]

Santiago, P. et al. (2016), *OECD Reviews of School Resources: Estonia 2016*, OECD Reviews of School Resources, OECD Publishing, Paris, http://dx.doi.org/10.1787/9789264251731-en. [12]

Skolverket and ReferNet Sweden (2016), *Vocational Education and Training: Sweden*, Cedefop ReferNet VET in Europe reports, https://cumulus.cedefop.europa.eu/files/vetelib/2016/2016_CR_SE.pdf. [14]

Stenström, M. and M. Virolainen (2014), *The Current State and Challenges of Vocational Education and Training in Finland*, Roskilde University. [29]

Swiss Coordination Centre for Research in Education (2014), *Swiss Education Report 2014*, http://skbf-csre.ch/fileadmin/files/pdf/bildungsmonitoring/Swiss_Education_Report_2014.pdf. [1]

World Bank (2012), *World Development Report 2013*, The World Bank, http://dx.doi.org/10.1596/978-0-8213-9575-2. [21]

Chapter 3. Pathways and progression for vocational education and training graduates in Estonia

For initial vocational education and training (VET) graduates in Estonia, many learning pathways are open in principle, but rarely travelled. The optional extra year of education that helps upper secondary VET graduates to qualify for higher education attracted very few students each year. This is a major challenge, since the prospect of progression is often the key tool to attract good candidates into the VET track. This chapter gives recommendations on facilitating progression beyond VET into higher education, on developing hybrid programmes within VET schools, and on further developing Estonia's already strong professional examination system.

The statistical data for Israel are supplied by and under the responsibility of the relevant Israeli authorities. The use of such data by the OECD is without prejudice to the status of the Golan Heights, East Jerusalem and Israeli settlements in the West Bank under the terms of international law.

Introduction

Opportunities for further education are vital for VET graduates

In the past, vocational education and training, in Estonia as in other countries, was primarily designed to train young people for an occupation that they would pursue throughout their working life. But this simple pattern now rarely holds. Rapid change in the labour market, driven by technology, is changing the skillsets required in many occupations, and eliminating some types of job, while also creating other, new job roles. Higher level skills are increasingly in demand. This means that the typical graduate of initial VET will need to upskill and/or reskill during their working lives (OECD, 2014[1]).

Changes in labour market demands are matched by growing aspirations

The aspiration to higher level qualifications is now nearly universal. For young people with such aspirations, the perception of general upper secondary education as the natural route to university represents formidable competition for any parallel vocational track. In Estonia as elsewhere, this means that the role of initial vocational education has to change. Rather than a dead end, it must be seen as a first step to lifelong learning. Partly this means ensuring that VET programmes, as well as meeting immediate employer needs, include sufficient general skills and education to facilitate further learning. These issues were discussed in Chapter 2. It also means ensuring that VET graduates have a full opportunity to progress into further and higher education. The pathways involved form the subject of this chapter.

A new UNESCO report spells out the importance of progression pathways

A new report from UNESCO (2018[2]) (Box 3.2) encourages the development of pathways from initial VET programmes to further and higher education. It argues that the development of such pathways serves multiple policy objectives, increasing the attractiveness of initial VET by meeting student aspirations, and removing any perception of VET tracks as dead-ends; helping to meet growing economic demands for higher level skills and qualifications; supporting lifelong learning; and removing wasteful barriers, such as requirements to repeat course material; and improving equity by promoting the access of more disadvantaged groups to higher level programmes. All of these points are relevant to Estonia. The more specific challenge faced by Estonia, which, as discussed in Chapter 2, sets it apart from some other European countries, is the relatively small size of the upper secondary VET sector, with relatively few high-performing students entering VET. This means that the challenge of establishing a well-travelled route from VET to more advanced programmes is often greater in Estonia than elsewhere.

The main challenges

Progression from upper secondary VET to higher education

In principle most pathways are open

Many countries with upper secondary VET tracks, and the Nordic countries particularly, have wrestled with the challenge of whether to permit those with upper secondary VET qualifications to proceed directly to higher education, typically through a common core of general education in both upper secondary and vocational tracks, assessed at the end of both tracks. Such direct access supports the status of the VET track, and its attractiveness. But at the same time it means that the VET track will need to be demanding academically, so as to prepare students for higher education, and this may promote drop out. This same dilemma was noted in Chapter 2 in relation to the attention given to basic skills in the course of VET programmes. Estonia permit access from vocational upper secondary programmes to higher education, but in practice higher education institutions are selective, and entrants are overwhelmingly from general education.

Few students pursue the additional bridging year to access higher education

Since 2006, an additional one-year bridging course,[1] focusing on theoretical subjects, has been available for upper secondary VET graduates who wish also to prepare for the state examination that grants access to higher education. But few students use it: in 2016 only 21 students started this bridging course, down from 50 in 2010 (Ministry of Education and Research, 2017[3]). For comparison, in Latvia for example, a similar one-year bridging programme enrolled around 15% of upper secondary VET students, or more than 200 of the students graduating from upper secondary VET in 2013/14 (OECD, 2016[4]).

There are two reasons why the bridging year attracts few takers in Estonia

First, as noted earlier in this report, upper secondary VET attracts few of the stronger school performers who might naturally expect to continue in higher education (i.e. those with high grade point averages). The second reason is that an extra year in school has a large opportunity cost, because of the wages VET graduates would otherwise receive. In addition, students while studying in ordinary upper secondary VET receive various benefits from the state as students, but they lose those benefits and social guarantees if they pursue the additional bridging year, unless they work. It is therefore unsurprising that a CEDEFOP survey found that 44% of respondents in Estonia said that it was difficult to switch from vocational to general education in their country (CEDEFOP, 2017[5]). First, as noted earlier in this report, upper secondary VET attracts few of the stronger.

Other progression from VET

Relatively few graduates from any VET programme proceed to the next level

More broadly, few graduates from the different VET programmes proceed to further programmes at a higher level, and many of those who do continue in education do so at the same level. This is true both of those in upper secondary VET programmes, and of those in post-secondary and level 5 programmes (Table 3.1). European Qualifications Framework (EQF) level 5 programmes are a relatively new innovation in Estonia (since 2013). But there is little evidence as yet that they serve as an important route for graduates of upper secondary VET.

Table 3.1. The status of students the following school year after completing a VET qualification

% (year)

	Not in education the following school year	In education EQF 4 or below	EQF 5 and post-secondary VET	Higher education
EQF 4 (ISCED 351)	81	7	6	6
EQF 4 (ISCED 354)	82	7	4	7
Post-secondary VET	83	5	4	8
EQF 5 (ISCED 454)	81	2	5	11

Source: Adapted from Ministry of Education and Research (2017[3]), *Background Report for OECD on Vocational Education and Training (VET) in Estonia*, www.hm.ee/sites/default/files/uuringud/oecd_vet_background.pdf

In Estonia, few VET graduates progress into professional bachelor's programmes

In principle, one might expect VET graduates to be natural candidates for professional programmes in technical universities of applied science (ISCED 1997 5B and ISCED 2011 6, EQF level 6). But in fact, in 2016-17, only 16% of students enrolled in these programmes came from vocational upper secondary education, (including some who studied unrelated occupations) with 80% coming from general upper secondary education. Higher education was made free of tuition fees in 2013, increasing the competition for limited numbers of study places, and therefore raising the threshold of academic attainment required to obtain entry (Ministry of Education and Research, 2017[6]). In ordinary bachelor's programmes, only 5% of students come from upper secondary VET. This contrasts with experience in some other countries such as Switzerland and the Netherlands, where half or more of the students in universities of applied science come from VET backgrounds. The positive experience in some fields in Norway is relevant, noting that this also involves some adjustment of first year university programmes to ensure that VET graduates receive extra support to develop their theoretical knowledge (Box 3.1).

Box 3.1. Course exemptions in higher education for vocational graduates in Norway

In Norway, some VET graduates can directly enter relevant bachelor programmes. These pathways are available from numerous VET fields of study, and especially within engineering. The students might have an alternative first year in university, often with more theoretical subjects instead of the more practical parts of the programme compared to the other students. Experience from the engineering programmes, which first started accepting VET graduates, have been successful. Reports state that companies often find students with a VET background to be more attractive. Accepting VET graduates into engineering degree programmes is now an important tool used to ensure that Norway trains enough engineers.

Source: NOKUT (2008[7]), *Evaluering av ingeniorutdanningen i Norge 2008, Norge. Del 1 hovedrapport*, www.nokut.no/Documents/NOKUT/Artikkelbibliotek/Norsk_utdanning/Evaluering/INGEVA/Rapporter/ING EVA_NOKUT_%20del%201%20Hovedrapport.pdf; Norwegian Ministry for Education and Research (2012[8]), *Meld. St. 13 (2011-2012) Utdanning for velferd, Norway*, www.regjeringen.no/no/dokumenter/meld-st-13-20112012/id672836/sec4.

Transitions from EQF level 5 programmes to higher education

Graduates from post-secondary VET programmes often wish to progress into linked higher education programmes. In Estonia, graduates of the new (since 2013) EQF level 5 qualification can be granted course exemptions for their previous training on entry to higher education, a right defined at the national level. But it is the individual higher education institution's privilege to assess the individual student and the use of exemptions is therefore variable. Such transitions are common in some countries: at any point in time, more than one in ten graduates of short-cycle professional programmes in Austria, Sweden and the United States are studying at tertiary level (Figure 3.1).

Figure 3.1. In some countries, post-secondary VET graduates often enter higher education

Percentage of graduates of post-secondary VET programmes aged 16-65 studying at tertiary level (5A or 5B)

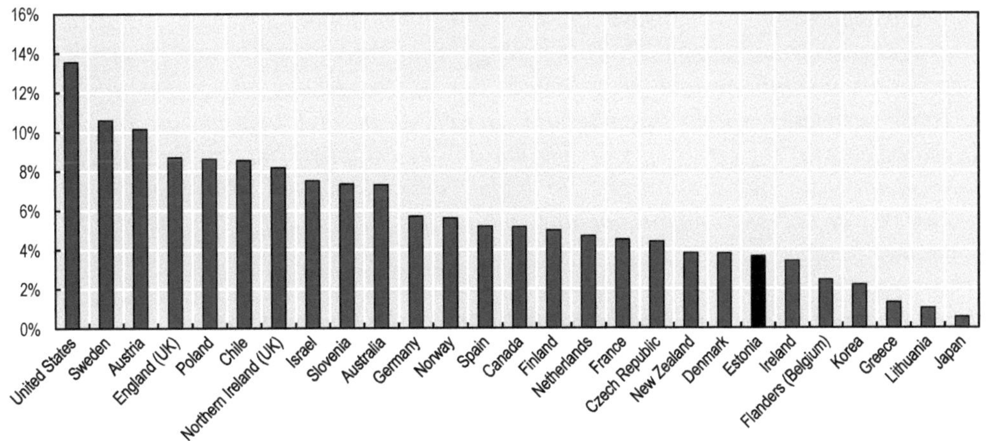

Source: Calculations based OECD (2015[9]), OECD Survey of Adult Skills (PIAAC) (Database 2012, 2015), www.oecd.org/site/piaac/publicdataandanalysis.htm.

StatLink https://doi.org/10.1787/888933921814

Recommendations

To address the challenges described, the following recommendations are advanced:

- Recommendation 3.1. Develop a multi-dimensional strategy to facilitate progression from initial VET. This strategy would recognise the need to work with different institutions and programmes across the education system, including career guidance within basic school as well as in VET institutions; building a dialogue with higher education institutions to establish the credentials of VET graduates as potential entrants to higher education; and addressing equity to ensure fair access to post-secondary and higher education by gender, region and mother tongue.

- Recommendation 3.2. Establish, within upper secondary VET, a hybrid programme to prepare students for the state examination offering access to higher education, as well as training them in their VET speciality. This approach would be designed to attract into VET more students with good school performance, and raise the status of VET in general.

- Recommendation 3.3. Building on the existing system of occupational examinations, further develop a higher-level examination system. This would follow the model of the dual system countries in providing higher level VET qualifications, particularly for working adults, for graduates of the initial VET system.

- Recommendation 3.4. Consider the option of a central fund, designed to target areas of specific skills shortage, and groups and regions with particular needs for reskilling, involving partnerships between employers and training providers, using the model of Swedish higher VET.

Analysis and supporting arguments

Establish a multi-dimensional strategy to facilitate progression.

Recommendation 3.1. Develop a multi-dimensional strategy to facilitate progression from initial VET. This strategy would recognise the need to work with different institutions and programmes across the education system, including career guidance within basic school as well as in VET institutions; building a dialogue with higher education institutions to establish the credentials of VET graduates as potential entrants to higher education; and addressing equity to ensure fair access to post-secondary and higher education by gender, region and mother tongue.

Many diverse factors potentially contribute to effective pathways

A very wide range of stakeholders are involved in pathways from VET to further and higher education. A new UNESCO report sets out a range of strategies, backed by country examples that may facilitate progression (Box 3.2). Guidance and information received by basic school students needs to indicate the prospects of progression (see Chapter 4). Initial VET programmes should prepare students for further learning, equipping them (as discussed in Chapter 2) with the range of basic and foundation skills that support further learning. Higher education institutions need to see that it is in their interest to adapt their provision so as to integrate entrants from the VET track, and partnerships between VET and higher education institutions need to be established to ensure mutual credit recognition.

A publicly announced strategy would give a higher profile to pathways

All of these factors need to act together, in a cycle of mutual reinforcement to facilitate progression, ensuring that there is a good fit between initiatives in one sector with those in another. To achieve this end, a focal point should be established within the Ministry of Education and Research to take ownership of a public strategy and co-ordinate the engagement of different bodies in these different initiatives. The existence of a public strategy will in itself be helpful in underlining the fact that upper secondary VET should no longer be seen as a dead end. Within this strategy it could also be guaranteed to vocational students that they would not lose their social benefits if they do the additional bridging year, as it is the case for the time-being.

> **Box 3.2. UNESCO recommendations for improving pathways between VET and further and higher education**
>
> To promote progression pathways through transparency, the report recommends using National Qualifications Frameworks to support transitions; supporting credit recognition agreements linked to learning outcomes; developing systems for recognising prior learning; and offering quality career guidance, backed by data on labour market outcomes, allowing VET students and graduates to identify options for further learning.
>
> To design initial VET to support lifelong learning, and augment it with bridges to more advanced programmes the report recommends building into initial VET programmes a sufficient range of general knowledge and skills, including study skills, literacy, numeracy and digital skills, into vocational programmes and qualifications, equipping graduates with the skills needed to learn throughout their life, formally and informally, and supporting access to further and higher education; and providing optional bridging programmes for VET students allowing them to access further and higher education.
>
> To remove the obstacles and fill the gaps in post-secondary provision the report recommends widening participation in higher and further education, thus allowing more access for VET graduates, broadening entrance criteria to give full recognition to VET and practitioner competences alongside academic skills; developing shorter post-secondary vocational programmes; and meeting the needs of adults through flexibility in time scheduling, and making full use of modern information and communications technology.
>
> *Source*: UNESCO (2018[21]), *Pathways of Progression: Between Technical and Vocational Education and Training and Further and Higher Education.*

The higher education community will need to be convinced of the strategy

Work with higher education institutions, individually and collectively, will be a critical part of the strategy, and potentially the most challenging. These institutions may not always welcome entrants with VET backgrounds, either because they believe that VET programmes have inadequately prepared students for the more academic demands of higher education, or because VET has come to signal low ability in the entrants to that track. But higher education can draw strength from a diversification of the student mix through an intake of vocationally trained students. While universities have always sought excellence, such excellence includes practical and vocational knowledge and skills, as well as more abstract and academic skills. Achieving this vision will require dialogue with the higher education community.

Enhance access to higher education from upper secondary VET

Recommendation 3.2. Establish, within upper secondary VET, a hybrid programme to prepare students for the state examination offering access to higher education, as well as training them in their VET speciality. This approach would be designed to attract into VET more students with good school performance, and raise the status of VET in general.

Hybrid programmes blend VET and general education

Many countries across Europe are establishing hybrid programmes, that offer from the outset within the frame of a single upper secondary programme, both a route to a vocational qualification and a qualification for entry into higher education (Deissinger et al., 2013[10]). The advantage of hybrid programmes is that they allow students to enter the VET track without abandoning the prospect of a direct route to higher education offered by general education. The disadvantage is that it is difficult to encompass, within a single manageable programme, both the requirements of a vocational specialty, and the general academic requirements to pass an exam to enter higher education. Many countries have felt the advantages outweigh the disadvantages, not least because hybrid programmes provide a powerful means of attracting into VET the stronger-performing students who are often attracted to higher education, and would, in the absence of the hybrid option, not consider entering the VET track.

In Estonia, a hybrid programme would attract high-performing students into VET

In Estonia, the arguments for a hybrid programme are compelling. Progression from upper secondary VET to higher education is low by international standards, and few of those with strong school attainment enter upper secondary VET. This suggests that there would be demand for a hybrid programme among those who currently pursue general upper secondary education. Experience with one hybrid programme – the Danish EUX programme – suggests that such programmes can effectively attract students with intermediate level school attainment (Box 3.3).

A hybrid programme would be demanding

Practically, such a hybrid programme, as in other countries, would have to handle the challenge of including both the general education and vocational requirements in a single programme. This would most likely mean a heavier workload and intensity of the programme relative to ordinary upper secondary VET, and partly some increase in its overall length relative to a standard VET programme. Different modes of study might be explored for the additional requirements – for example through evening, weekend and holiday courses, and different forms of e-learning, so as to be fitted around the normal routine of a VET programme.

> **Box 3.3. The EUX hybrid programme in Denmark**
>
> The EUX programme was launched in Denmark in 2010 as a means of improving the attractiveness of VET by encouraging the link between VET and higher education. EUX combines a three-year gymnasium general upper secondary education and a four-year apprenticeship in a single programme. EUX is normally four years and a few months in length, with some variability between fields of study. It is a demanding programme, since the students must follow two curricula, so it will only become a small part of the Danish VET system (2% of students in 2013-14). An evaluation has shown that it can attract a group of mid-performing students into VET. These are students with a stronger academic performance than most VET students, but not as strong as the strongest gymnasium students.
>
> *Source*: Ramboll (2017[11]), *Evaluering af EUX – endelig rapport*, www.dpt.dk/wp-content/uploads/2010/06/170315-Evaluering-af-eux.pdf; Jørgensen, C. (2015[12]), *Recent Innovations in VET in Denmark. Responses to Key Challenges for VET*, http://nord-vet.dk/indhold/uploads/report1c_dk.pdf.

International experience could guide the Estonian approach

Switzerland, for example, has been relatively successful at opening the technical universities of applied science to vocational graduates, through a special optional general education qualification (*Berufsmaturität*) that provides access to tertiary education. This qualification can be pursued alongside regular upper secondary apprenticeship through one day a week of study. More than 10% of VET students now obtain this qualification, and VET graduates now represent around half of the students in the universities of applied science (Nikolai and Ebner, 2011[13]; Hoeckel, Field and Grubb, 2009[14]).

Develop a higher level examination system

> *Recommendation 3.3. Building on the existing system of occupational examinations, further develop a higher level examination system. This would follow the model of the dual system countries in providing higher level VET qualifications, particularly for working adults, for graduates of the initial VET system.*

Estonia already has a well-structured system of occupational examinations

Estonia's established system of occupational qualifications and examinations has great strengths, rooted as it is in sector skills councils which construct the qualifications in line with labour market needs and an established framework for managing the examinations, by franchising an examination body for five years to undertake each examination. The examinations are flexible, such that they are applicable to those who have completed a formal programme of study, for example in upper secondary VET, as well as to those who have acquired their occupational skills more informally, and wish to have them formally certified through the examination.

In several countries professional examinations play a key role in progression from the initial VET system

In the dual system countries in particular, professional examinations are widely used as a means of providing higher level vocational skills in individual professions to graduates of the initial VET system (see Box 3.4 for an example from Germany). Typically graduates in a vocational field, after some years of working in that field, might pursue the examination. These examinations serve an important role, alongside other pathways of progression for vocational graduates.

Box 3.4. Advanced vocational examinations in Germany

Advanced vocational examinations are typically pursued after the completion of upper secondary vocational training (such as apprenticeship) and some years of relevant work experience, and reflect the classical progression from apprentice to Meister. Meister examinees must show that they can pursue their profession independently, run their own business and can train apprentices. These qualifications are now available, not only in technical professions but also in agricultural, commercial, manufacturing, and service-related sectors. The certified senior clerk (*Fachwirt/in*) rose in popularity by 45% between 2003 and 2010 to become the most common advanced vocational examination, followed by the certified industrial supervisor (*Industriemeister*) and the master of skilled trade (*Handwerkmeister*). The federal and the chamber regulations define admission requirements, examination arrangements and pass criteria. Boards of experienced examiners include equal numbers from the employers' and the employees' side and at least one vocational school teacher. Preparatory courses for examinations are not mandatory, but candidates almost always attend either part- or full-time courses offered by the chambers or private providers (of which there are over 15 000).

Source: OECD (2014[11]), *Skills beyond School: Synthesis Report*, OECD Reviews of Vocational Education and Training, http://dx.doi.org/10.1787/9789264214682-en.

In Estonia, the occupational examinations can be used to upskill

The OECD team were told that it is already possible in Estonia to use these examinations as a means of upskilling graduates of the initial VET system. Unfortunately, this route is not extensively publicised, and not used extensively. These higher level vocational qualifications are neither widely recognised nor well rewarded in the labour market. Individuals have to pay for these examinations and any preparatory training that they need to undertake these examinations. By way of comparison, in Switzerland, 60-80% of the costs of this type of examination are paid by government (Swiss Confederation, 2016[15]).

The use of higher level professional examinations could be promoted

For adult graduates of initial vocational education, higher level professional examinations have much to offer. These graduates will usually be in employment and therefore need programmes of further learning that can recognise their work experience, and build on it in a flexible way through evening or weekend courses consistent with work and family responsibilities. This will usually be a more practical and efficient way of developing their professional career than a full-time, or even a part-time regular education and training programme. Estonia might therefore usefully promote such programmes. Practical steps might include providing some funding subsidy in support of these examinations, as in Switzerland. A clear recognisable name for such examinations/qualifications would also help to establish their profile and visibility. In Switzerland they correspond to Swiss Federal Diplomas and Advanced Swiss Federal Diplomas. The Meister title is also used for some of these examinations in the German-speaking countries.

Consider the option of a central fund to support specific skills needs

> *Recommendation 3.4 Consider the option of a central fund, designed to target areas of specific skills shortage, and groups and regions with particular needs for reskilling, involving partnerships between employers and training providers, using the model of Swedish higher VET.*

One risk in the Estonian VET system is that provision may not match labour market need

The new OSKA measures of labour market requirements should, in principle, guide the mix of upper secondary VET provision, but this is limited by pressure to offer students their choice of fields of study, partly out of an understandable concern that if they do not obtain their choice, they might drop out. At post-secondary and higher education level, student choice is often the key driver of provision. This means that there are risks that the VET system will not be sufficiently responsive to emerging skills shortages, in a context in which employer surveys suggest that such shortages are often a key barrier to growth (OECD, 2017[16]).

A central fund might help to tackle skills shortages

Alongside the risk of specific skills shortages, often in particular regions, some groups of adults may need upskilling and reskilling. One way of handling such specific skills gaps would be to establish a central fund to address them. The fund would support partnerships between training providers (which could be a variety of institutions) and employers to deliver specific occupational qualifications identified as being in shortage. This would follow the successful Swedish model of higher vocational education (Box 3.5). In each case it would be up to the partners to provide a planned programme to deliver the skills required for the occupational examination. The costs of the examinations would also be met from this fund.

Box 3.5. The Swedish system of higher vocational education (HVE)

Higher vocational education (HVE) was established in 2001 with enrolment increasing rapidly to reach 31 000 (compared with 140 000 enrolments in professional bachelors and masters programmes). Most programmes require between six months and two years of full-time study with 70% of programmes lasting two years. There is demand from students, support by employers, and interest among bodies wishing to run courses. 80-90% of graduates report being in work one year after graduation. Many different bodies can provide HVE if they comply with the established requirements. In 2011, out of 242 institutions providing HVE, roughly half were private while the rest belonged to local and regional authorities. All HVE programmes are publicly funded, with no tuition fees. The model fosters a bottom-up and entrepreneurial approach within a publicly funded framework. Workplace training is obligatory in two-year HVE programmes and represents one-quarter of the programme duration.

This structure builds partnership with employers into the design of the system, since it is only possible to seek funding for an HVE programme when a partnership with employers willing to offer the workplace training is already in place. Each HVE programme has a steering group including employers: employers provide training to students and advise on provision and programme content. To launch a programme an education provider has to show that there is labour market demand for the skills provided by the programme, and that it has a framework to engage employers. The National Agency for Higher VET is responsible for the sector, and the social partners are part of a council that advises the agency on the future demand for skills and on how this might be met.

Source: Kuczera, M. (2013[17]), *A Skills beyond School Commentary on Sweden*, www.oecd.org/edu/skills-beyond-school/ASkillsBeyondSchoolCommentaryOnSweden.pdf, Ministry of Education and Research Sweden (2013[18]), *Background Report from Sweden, Skills beyond School*, www.oecd.org/edu/skills-beyond-school/SkillsBeyondSchoolSwedishBackgroundReport.pdf.

Note

[1] The optional extra year is not mandatory for entering higher education. It is simply an opportunity to prepare for state examinations that take place at the end of upper secondary education and that are required by some higher education institutions. Upper secondary VET students can also prepare for state examinations during the course of their studies by selecting non-compulsory general subjects.

References

CEDEFOP (2017), *Cedefop European Public Opinion Survey on Vocational Education and Training*, Publications Office of the European Union, Luxembourg. [5]

Deissinger, T. et al. (2013), "Hybrid qualifications: Structures and problems in the context of European VET policy", *Studies in Vocational and Continuing Education*, Vol. 10. [10]

Hoeckel, K., S. Field and W. Grubb (2009), *OECD Reviews of Vocational Education and Training: A Learning for Jobs Review of Switzerland 2009*, OECD Reviews of Vocational Education and Training, OECD Publishing, Paris, https://dx.doi.org/10.1787/9789264113985-en. [14]

Jørgensen, C. (2015), *Recent Innovations in VET in Denmark. Responses to Key Challenges for VET*, Nord-VET – The future of Vocational Education in the Nordic countries, Roskilde, http://nord-vet.dk/indhold/uploads/report1c_dk.pdf. [12]

Kuczera, M. (2013), *A Skills beyond School Commentary on Sweden*, OECD Reviews of Vocational Education and Training, OECD Publishing, Paris, http://www.oecd.org/edu/skills-beyond-school/ASkillsBeyondSchoolCommentaryOnSweden.pdf. [17]

Ministry of Education and Research (2017), *Background Report for OECD on Vocational Education and Training (VET) in Estonia*, http://www.hm.ee/sites/default/files/uuringud/oecd_vet_background.pdf. [3]

Ministry of Education and Research (2017), *Higher Education, Estonia*, https://www.hm.ee/en/activities/higher-education. [6]

Ministry of Education and Research Sweden (2013), *Background Report from Sweden. Skills beyond School*, http://www.oecd.org/edu/skills-beyond-school/SkillsBeyondSchoolSwedishBackgroundReport.pdf. [18]

Nikolai, R. and C. Ebner (2011), "The link between vocational training and higher education in Switzerland, Austria, and Germany", in *The Political Economy of Collective Skill Formation*, Oxford University Press, http://dx.doi.org/10.1093/acprof:oso/9780199599431.003.0009. [13]

NOKUT (2008), *Evaluering av Ingeniorutdanningen i Norge 2008, Norge. Del 1 Hovedrapport*, (Evaluation of the Engineering Education in Norway 2008, Norway. Part 1 Main Report), http://www.nokut.no/Documents/NOKUT/Artikkelbibliotek/Norsk_utdanning/Evaluering/INGEVA/Rapporter/INGEVA_NOKUT_%20del%201%20Hovedrapport.pdf. [7]

Norwegian Ministry for Education and Research (2012), *Meld. St. 13 (2011-2012) Utdanning for velferd, Norway*, https://www.regjeringen.no/no/dokumenter/meld-st-13-20112012/id672836/sec4. [8]

OECD (2017), *OECD Economic Surveys: Estonia 2017*, OECD Publishing, Paris, http://dx.doi.org/10.1787/eco_surveys-est-2017-en. [16]

OECD (2016), *Education in Latvia*, Reviews of National Policies for Education, OECD Publishing, Paris, http://dx.doi.org/10.1787/9789264250628-en. [4]

OECD (2015), *OECD Survey of Adult Skills (PIAAC) (Database 2012, 2015)*, http://www.oecd.org/skills/piaac/publicdataandanalysis/. [9]

OECD (2014), *Skills beyond School: Synthesis Report*, OECD Reviews of Vocational Education and Training, OECD Publishing, Paris, http://dx.doi.org/10.1787/9789264214682-en. [1]

Ramboll (2017), *Evaluering af EUX – Endelig Rapport*, http://www.dpt.dk/wp-content/uploads/2010/06/170315-Evaluering-af-eux.pdf. [11]

Swiss Confederation (2016), *Vocational and Professional Education and Training in Switzerland Facts and Figures 2016*, https://www.eda.admin.ch/dam/countries/countries-content/canada/en/Vocational-and-professional-education-and-training-switzerland_E.pdf. [15]

UNESCO (2018), *Pathways of Progression: Between Technical and Vocational Education and Training and Further and Higher Education*, UNESCO, Paris. [2]

Chapter 4. Strengthening career guidance in Estonia

In Estonia, career guidance and information services have been extensively reorganised, and the system now has many strengths, but some gaps remain. Some of the elements of career guidance should be made mandatory in basic schools and provision should start early. Mandatory provision helps to ensure that the guidance gets through to some of the students who need it most. This in itself would provide a firmer foundation for decisions about whether to pursue a vocational education and training (VET) or general education track at grade 9. More accessible and understandable labour market information, including data from destinations surveys, would also be very helpful. Students would also benefit from visits to schools by people from different professional background, visits to workplaces by students, and short work placements and work shadowing.

Introduction

The growing importance of career guidance

In Estonia, as across the OECD, the decisions that young people need to make about their education and training are more difficult. This chapter focuses on career education, information and counselling (shortened to career guidance). The chapter recognises the many strengths of Estonian career guidance provision, while highlighting the importance of greater intervention: career guidance should ensure that all young people have a reasonable opportunity to consider the range of opportunities available to them, including those presented by vocational education and training, at an early stage.

Career guidance often works

Career guidance covers a wide range of activities but comparatively few studies have sought to apply experimental and quasi-experimental methodologies. A literature review undertaken by Hughes et al. in 2016 looked at the results of 73 studies on the impact of career guidance on economic, educational and social outcomes published since 1996. The review found that approximately two-thirds of studies revealed evidence of positive effects in terms of the three outcomes.[1] Very few studies revealed evidence of negative outcomes. Improvements in economic outcomes are better attributed to changes in career thinking and confidence in pathways pursued than in "employability" skills (Hughes et al., 2016[1]). While positive outcomes related to career guidance activities cannot be taken for granted, it is very difficult to find a reliable study that suggests interventions were a complete waste of time and had negative consequences for young people (Musset and Mytna Kurekova, 2018[2]).

The main challenges

Young Estonians may face difficulties entering the labour market

In Estonia in 2016, young people experienced unemployment rates twice the level of prime age adults, a ratio similar to many other countries (Figure 4.1). Such figures reflect the character of labour market demand, the limited experience of young people and the weaknesses of their social networks linked to employment.

Young people need to have good career management skills

Young people have, of course, long been at such a disadvantage within the labour market, in Estonia and in general in OECD countries. In Estonia as in other countries young people are entering a world of work which is undergoing rapid change. Technology is transforming jobs and the labour market is becoming more polarised by skills level with growth in high and certain low skill employment and a contraction of middle-skilled jobs. Switching between jobs and even economic sectors becomes more usual, and self-employment more commonplace (ILO, 2016[3]). The need for career management skills grows (Musset and Mytna Kurekova, 2018[2]; Neary, Hooley and Dodd, 2015[4]). It is a strength of the Estonian approach to career guidance that this need is recognised within provision (Ministry of Education and Research, 2017[5]).

Skills mismatch is also a challenge

Connected to the point made above, evidence gathered at the EU level shows that in Estonia while 33% of men and 27% of women are well matched (in terms of education and skills) for their job, 34% and 35% are mismatched in terms of education, and 16% and 17% are by skills (Flisi et al., 2016[6]). While long-term consequences remain to be seen, such mismatch is associated with lower than expected wages and job satisfaction. In Estonia, like in all countries which were part of this analysis, women are less likely to be matched than their male counterparts.

Figure 4.1. Young people (15-24) face higher unemployment than prime-age adults (25-54) in Estonia

Percentage of unemployment in the labour force, 2016

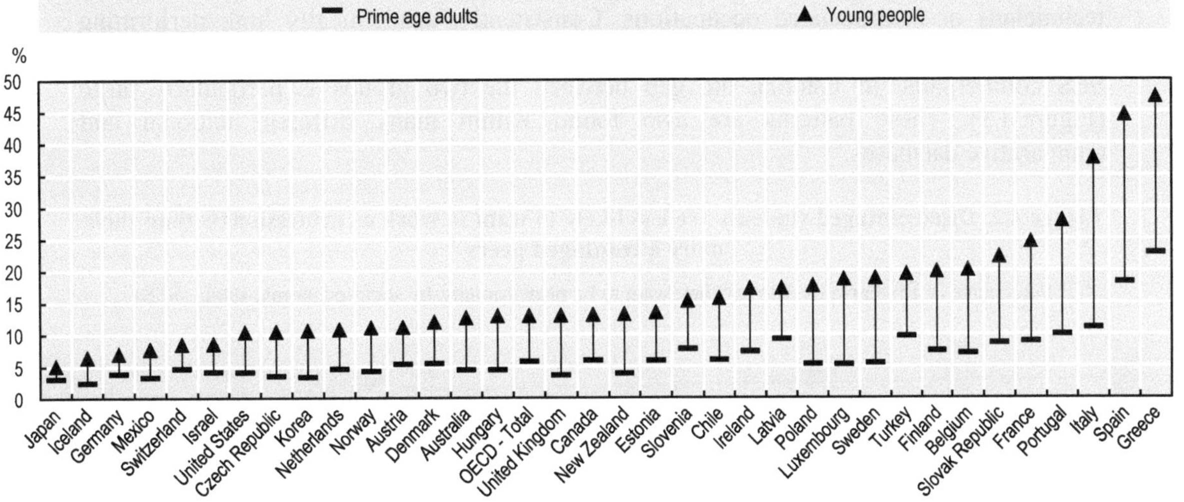

Source: OECD (2017[7]), "Unemployment rates by age", *OECD.Stat*, https://stats.oecd.org.

StatLink https://doi.org/10.1787/888933921833

Young people are often uninformed about the labour market and the implications of their educational choices

Career choices are closely tied in with educational choices which act as gateways to continuing study and often progression into careers of choice. Studies suggest that improved employment outcomes by career guidance are driven by increased student motivation linked to deeper understanding of the relationship between education and employment (Hughes et al., 2016[1]). In Estonia, like in other countries, the labour market outcomes that programme graduates can expect vary according to the type of programme and the field of study (Figure 4.6). Where information about labour market outcomes is not viewed as relevant by young people, young people can have a harder time making well informed decisions. In Estonia, as the point will be development later in this chapter, many people enter VET after having completed university, which shows career indecisions, and perhaps a lack of information about VET options and their outcomes, pointing towards inadequate and/or insufficient career guidance. Some students may not have the pre-requisites required to pursue the study programme that would lead to their preferred career either because they cannot achieve them or because they have closed off their options, for example, by not being able to pass the state entrance examination needed to enter higher education.

Some students may need more career guidance than others

Social and personal circumstances shape career thinking. Analysis from the Programme for International Student Assessment (PISA) data show that in Estonia, 58% of advantaged students, but only 36% of their less advantaged peers, want to work as professionals (Figure 4.2). Importantly, this statistically significant relationship between socio-economic status (SES) and career aspiration applies even when taking account of academic proficiency as measured in performance in the 2015 PISA tests on mathematics (Musset and Mytna Kurekova, 2018[2]). This means that some students may not reach their potential and may choose a future occupation within a limited set of options. Similar patterns are found in terms of the aspirations of young people from lower SES to work as technicians or in associated occupations. Consistently, academically high performing students from lower SES backgrounds are less ambitious for their futures than their high SES counterparts. In Estonia, the gap between the two groups is particularly large (Figure 4.3). These patterns are also found within many different national and comparative databases.[2]

Figure 4.2. Disadvantaged students are less likely to want to work as professionals than their more advantaged peers

Percentage of 15-year-olds who say they want to be professionals, by socio-economic status (SES)

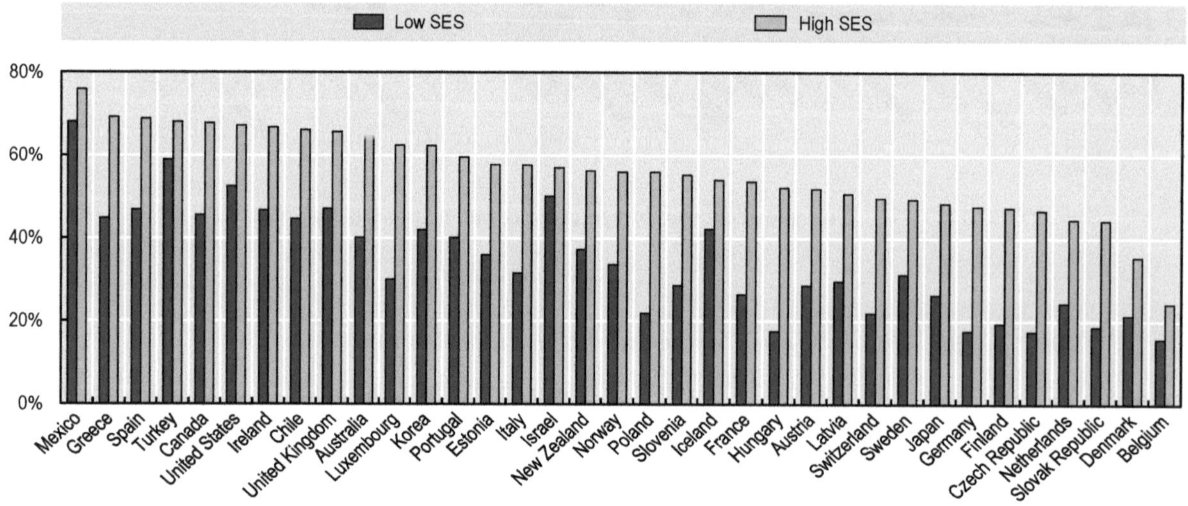

Note: No data are available for the Slovak Republic. Occupations classified as professionals include, for example, civil engineers, secondary school teachers, medical practitioners, and computer systems analysts. *Countries are sorted by highest percentage point difference.*
Source: Musset, P. and L. Mytna Kurekova (2018[2]), "Working it out: Career guidance and employer engagement", *OECD Education Working Papers*, No. 175, http://dx.doi.org/10.1787/51c9d18d-en.

StatLink https://doi.org/10.1787/888933921852

Figure 4.3. Disadvantaged students are less likely to want to go to universities

Difference in academic expectations between high SES and low SES students

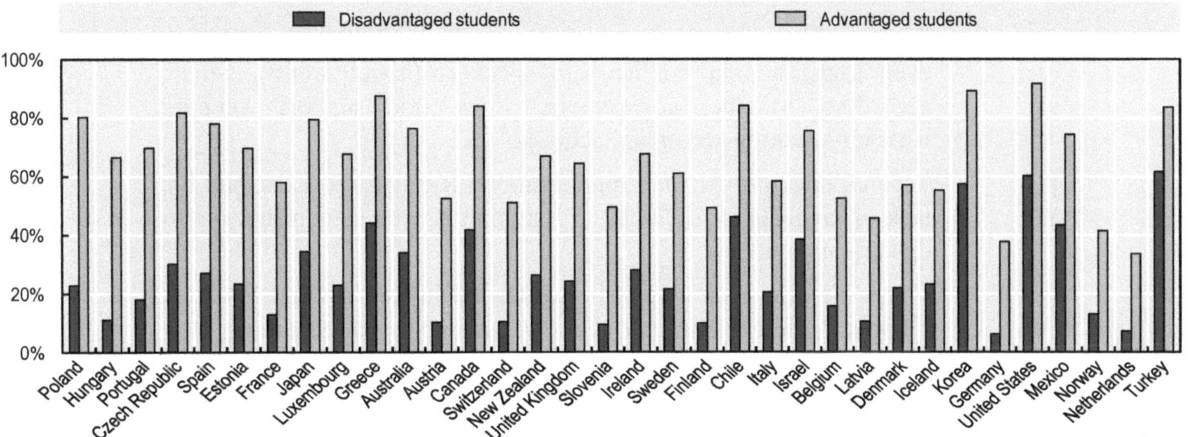

Note. No data are available for the Slovak Republic.
Countries are sorted by highest percentage point difference.
Source: Musset, P. and L. Mytna Kurekova (2018[2]), "Working it out: Career guidance and employer engagement", *OECD Education Working Papers*, No. 175, http://dx.doi.org/10.1787/51c9d18d-en.

StatLink ᐧᒥᔑ https://doi.org/10.1787/888933921871

Personal circumstances shape education and career thinking

Such patterns in educational expectation and participation are also found with respect to ethnicity, gender and geographic location. As discussed in earlier chapters, Russian-speakers are over-represented in VET provision, with 60% of Russian-speaking boys in north-eastern Estonia enrolled (Ministry of Education and Research, 2017[5]). Russian-speaking students are also under-represented in higher education (Lindemann and Saar, 2012[8]). There are diverse reasons why Russian speaking students are over-represented in VET: some argue that VET education is more valued among Russians, because many students are from families in which parents have a VET education themselves.[3] Pärtel and Petti (2013[9]) and Mägi and Nestor (2012[10]) looked at the factors influencing the choice of upper secondary tracks in Estonia, in differences between girls and boys, and between Russian-speakers and Estonian-speakers, as well as elements such as parental education and socio-economic background.

Box 4.1. Estonian language instruction and Russian language in Estonia

The views and actions of policy makers in Estonia regarding minority students' education are supported by research on second-language acquisition. The discussion in Estonia does not merely emphasise exposure to the Estonian language. Mother-tongue education until the end of the ninth grade with teaching of Estonian as a second language is the mainstream option for all students. But in upper secondary VET, Russian language teaching has not been phased out yet, contrary to the general education equivalent. In such programmes, 60% of the subjects are taught in Estonian and 40% in Russian.

Plans to phase out Russian language instruction at the secondary level go back to early 2000. The multiple reasons as reported by Kemppainen and Ellis Ferrin (2002) were:

- First, the birth rates are low in Estonia (about 12 000 annually) and even lower among the Russian speakers (about 3 000), which, according to the government, does not support keeping Russian-speaking secondary schools.

- Second, unemployment is higher among Russian speakers, and the lack of language proficiency in Estonian is seen as contributing to this unemployment.

- Third, the discipline emphasis is different in Russian and Estonian schools. Whereas Russian schools emphasise mathematics, their level of foreign-language teaching is low.

- Fourth, higher education in Estonia functions in the Estonian language.

However, some worries were expressed by the authorities regarding the non-Estonian language children who study in Estonian schools because of possible lower academic performance and the need to preserve the cultural identity of Russian speaking children. Other concerns involve the quality of educational attainment of Estonian children in a situation where teachers are not fully trained to deal with multilingual classes and the issues minority language students bring to Estonian-language schools.

Research suggests that exposure to the second language alone does not bring linguistic and academic success and that the process of learning a language at an academically functioning level can take five to seven or eight years.

Source: Kemppainen, R. and S. Ferrin Ellis (2002[11]), "Parental choice and language-of-instruction policies and practices in Estonia", *Education and Urban Society,* Vol. 35/1, pp.76-9.

Gender also shapes education and career aspirations

Girls in Estonia tend to have higher aspirations than boys and achieve just as well as boys, but receive lower wages as young women. In part, the gap is explained by the educational choices made by male and female students. Such decisions are likely to be shaped by assumptions about what employment it is reasonable for men and women to undertake in the workplace. Gender stereotypes are more prevalent in Estonia than in the average Western European country (Figure 4.4). It is noteworthy that among boys and girls from the same SES background and the same proficiency levels, it is girls who have the higher career expectations (Figure 4.5).

An important purpose of career guidance, therefore, is to provide young people from all backgrounds with relevant information and experiences in order to broaden and, potentially, to raise aspirations. This could help break intergenerational cycles of disadvantage (Musset and Mytna Kurekova, 2018[2]).

The labour market implications can be profound

While Estonian girls perform very well in relation to boys in PISA tests, soon after entry to the labour market, as set out in Figure 4.6 the earnings of young women are consistently lower than those enjoyed by young men. This earnings penalty is on average higher when comparing men and women with VET qualifications (41%) than when comparing men and women with higher education (34%). An important aspect of these earnings differentials relate to the programmes of study undertaken by young people prior to labour market entry.

Figure 4.4. Gender stereotypes are pronounced

Percentage of respondents who agreed with the statements below

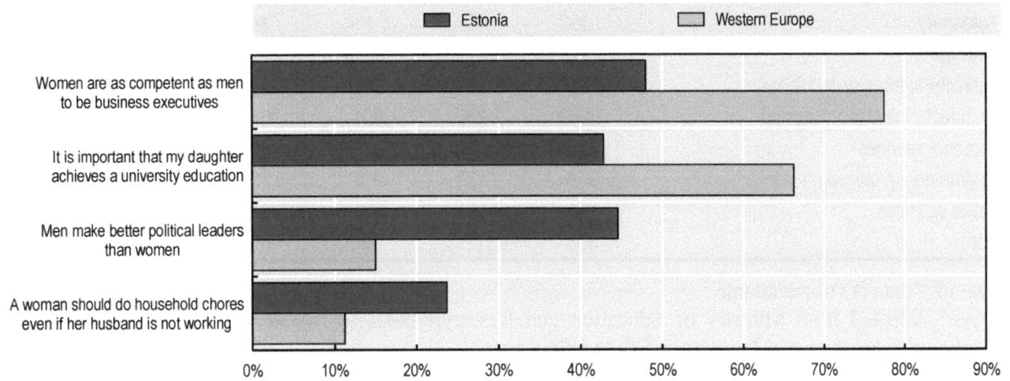

Source: OECD (2017[12]), *OECD Economic Surveys: Estonia 2017*, https://doi.org/10.1787/eco_surveys-est-2017-en.

StatLink https://doi.org/10.1787/888933921890

Figure 4.5. Girls have higher career aspirations than boys

Odds for girls expecting to work in skilled professions, over the odds for boys

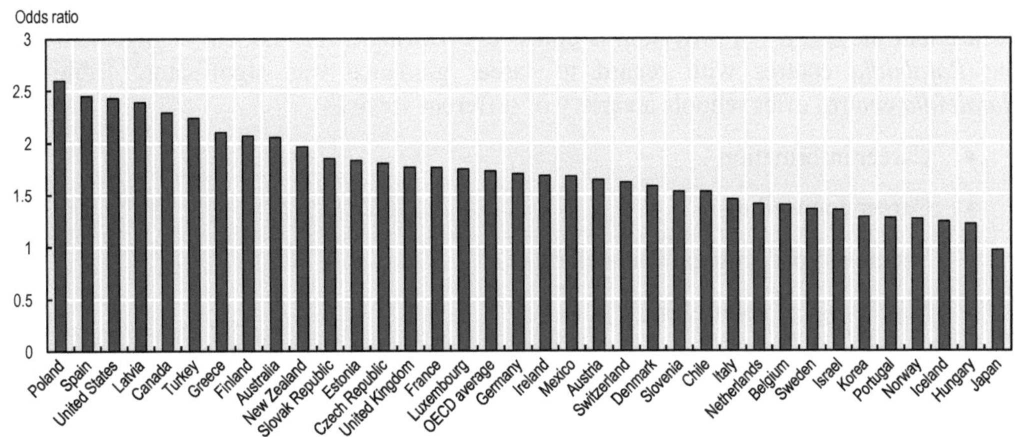

Note: After accounting for student characteristics and performance in mathematics.
Source: Musset, P. and L. Mytna Kurekova (2018[2]), "Working it out: Career guidance and employer engagement", *OECD Education Working Papers*, No. 175, http://dx.doi.org/10.1787/51c9d18d-en.

StatLink https://doi.org/10.1787/888933921909

Table 4.1. Labour market outcomes of different higher education and VET tracks, by field of study

Graduates from higher education and VET in 2005-13, their average income (in EUR) in 2014, by VET fields of study and gender

Field of study	Higher education			VET		
	Total	Male	Female	Total	Male	Female
ICT	1 713	1 777	1 500	881	982	653
Security services	1 530	1 600	1 268	1 130	1 174	989
Transportation services	1 480	1 618	1 274	767	929	590
Engineering specialties	1 451	1 495	1 205	897	913	616
Architecture and construction	1 307	1 442	1 055	773	792	543
Health	1 236	1 641	1 201	653	972	624
Business and management	1 204	1 405	1 133	702	885	676
Veterinary	1 198	1 428	1 154	740	m	740
Average	**1 176**	**1 425**	**1 060**	**772**	**887**	**622**
Agriculture, forestry and fishery	1 064	1 201	896	829	853	695
Manufacturing and processing	1 060	1 296	951	656	778	565
Personal services	974	1 073	937	620	761	574
Environmental protection	974	1 135	906	707	863	647
Social sciences	901	1 153	886	638	1 040	612
Arts	807	922	767	677	811	598

Note: m = data are not available.
Source: Adapted from Ministry of Education and Research (2017[5]), *Background Report for OECD on Vocational Education and Training (VET) in Estonia*, www.hm.ee/sites/default/files/uuringud/oecd_vet_background.pdf.

Career guidance in Estonia has improved but some challenges remain

Career guidance underwent a major and welcome change in 2014-15. Before 2014, guidance services were provided by a range of different institutions from both public and third sectors resulting in a service which was recognised as fragmented and uneven. Career guidance services are now provided by sixteen youth guidance centres (*Rajaleidja*) located in every county. The centres operate within a unified quality assurance system and have adopted common procedures and standards in an attempt to ensure that the quality of provision is consistent. During 2017, student engagement with the *Rajaleidja* centres with regard to career guidance was significant (Table 4.2). *Rajaleidja* centres offer schools a variety of different services:

- Career information
- Career counselling
- Social and pedagogical counselling
- Psychological counselling
- Special education counselling
- Speech therapy.

Table 4.2. Number of participants in services organised by Rajaleidja centres

2017

Types of activities	Number
Number of students who have received individual career services	30 710
Number of students who have received individual educational counselling	17 309
Number of teachers and parents who have received individual counselling	3 878
Number of participants in group counselling sessions	150 141

Source: Adapted from Foundation Innove (2018[13]), *Lifelong Guidance in Estonia*, www.innove.ee/en/.

Consolidation of the Estonian career guidance system has been positive

The recent consolidation of career guidance delivery is recognition of the importance with which such services are viewed in Estonia, and provides a strong foundation for provision. The profession of guidance counsellor is clearly and appropriately structured (Foundation Innove, 2018[14]). Provision acknowledges, and to some extent addresses, the importance of parents as influencers of young people. Employers are also actively engaged in delivery. With guidance located in regional centres, impartiality can be expected to be less of a concern than in countries where it is schools which fully deliver provision.

However, the service also faces a significant challenge

Following the spirit of school autonomy, it is schools and teachers who are responsible for organising career guidance activities and this has led to large variation in practice. Some schools engage actively in the offer and ensure that students engage in counselling sessions, visit job fairs and other exploratory activities including rich engagement with employers. Others do not or do so in an inconsistent fashion. The Foundation Innove reports that fewer than half of young people in grades 7 to 9 receive individual career services as do fewer than one in ten of students enrolled in vocational schools (Foundation Innove, 2018[13]). This partial take-up of the guidance offer raises concerns. Opportunity exists for a clearer statement of what all young Estonians should be able to expect in terms of guidance support. The goal is that in Estonia lifelong learning strategy, by 2020, 100% of basic school graduates have had career guidance (Ministry of Education and Research, 2014[15]).

There are concerns that guidance services are uneven

Whilst in Estonia, the project team heard concerns over the unevenness of career guidance provision, and there is reason to believe that provision requires further improvement: nearly one in five (18%) higher education graduates ultimately end up in VET provision; the average age of graduation for post-secondary VET is 29, much higher than in other OECD countries. Combined with high levels of NEET figures related to VET provision, a picture emerges of school-to-work transitions which are unduly fragmented and inefficient for both the individual and to society.

The importance of effective career guidance for VET provision

In many countries, there is a specific need for career guidance services to ensure that young people have an informed understanding of what VET has to offer. This is particularly the case where VET has a poor historical reputation and where the (often unspoken and often socially conditioned) assumptions of young people and parents have failed to keep pace with meaningful changes in the quality of actual provision. In Estonia, PISA surveys record, by way of example, a falling interest in professions to which VET is commonly a gateway. In keeping with the pattern of rising aspirations noted earlier, there has been a large fall in the proportion of Estonian teenagers expecting to follow a career in semi-skilled employment (Figure 4.6). Career guidance, particularly where informed by labour market realities, and delivered from an early age in the school lives, can help challenge such assumptions. This is particularly important where students are required to switch schools in order to pursue VET programmes – as is often the case in Estonia. Such students need especially careful counselling as specific VET programmes can effectively place limits on future progression due to a narrowing of the curriculum (Musset and Mytna Kurekova, 2018[2]).

Figure 4.6. In many countries relatively few young people expect to have a manual job

The jobs that 15-year-olds expect to have by age 30: percentage expecting to have semi-skilled manual jobs (ISCO 6-8 categories)

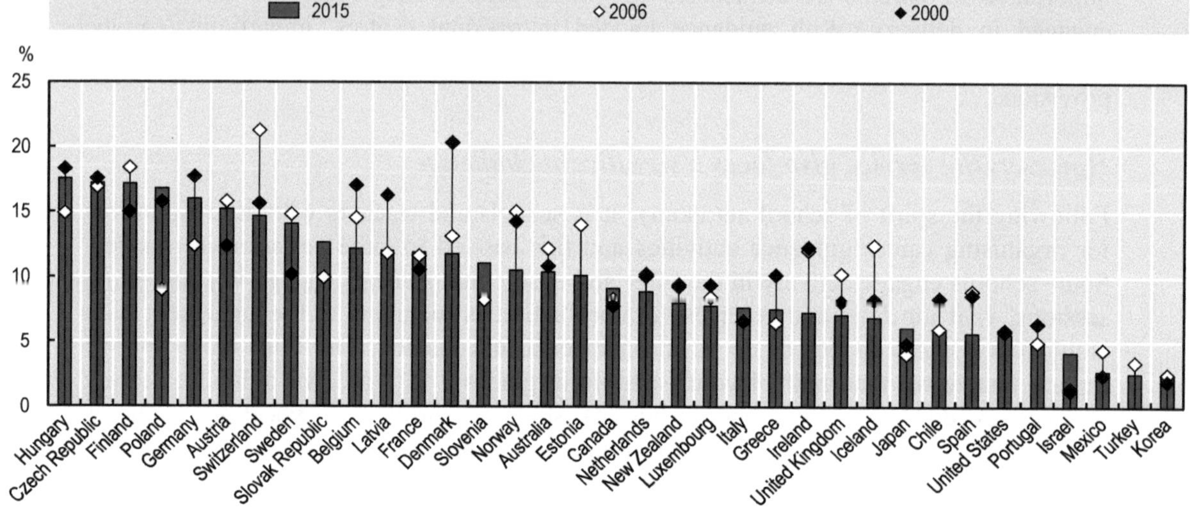

Note: ISCO 6-8 categories include skilled agricultural, forestry and fishery workers; craft and related trades workers; plant and machine operators, and assemblers.
Source: Musset, P. and L. Mytna Kurekova (2018[2]),"Working it out: Career guidance and employer engagement", *OECD Education Working Papers*, No. 175, http://dx.doi.org/10.1787/51c9d18d-en.

StatLink https://doi.org/10.1787/888933921928

Recommendations

To address the challenges described, the following recommendations are advanced:

- Recommendation 4.1. Make some of the elements of the career guidance provision mandatory, in particular before grade 9, in all schools and in all classrooms, and monitor student participation to ensure that this goal is reached.

- Recommendation 4.2. Enhance use of data in career guidance, introducing destination surveys.

- Recommendation 4.3. Make sure that students get multiple opportunities to interact with people in work and workplaces.

Analysis and supporting arguments

Make some of the elements of the career guidance provision mandatory

Recommendation 4.1. Make some of the elements of the career guidance provision mandatory, in particular before grade 9, in all schools and in all classrooms, and monitor student participation to ensure that this goal is reached.

Career guidance activities should begin young

Effective career guidance will begin young (in some forms in pre-primary and primary schooling) and intensify in the run up to key transition points. Even before starting school, children already have some awareness of jobs and are beginning to form views about whether particular types of work are likely to be for them or not. Such assumptions are commonly rooted in social contexts and can lead to young students ruling out certain professions (and programmes of study) from an early age with long lasting implications (Archer et al., 2013[16]). Consequently, career guidance activities should begin from primary school, and aim at broadening the interests and aspirations of children, allowing them to see the links between what they do in school and who they might ultimately become in the workplace (Watson and McMahon, 2005[17]). This can prevent stereotypical thinking from guiding the decision making of students (Howard et al., 2015[18]). The new Careers Strategy of the Department for Education in England (United Kingdom), for example, highlights the importance of career-related provision and employer engagement within primary education (Department for Education, 2017[19]) and see also Wade et al. (2011[20]) for the evaluation of career-related learning aimed at children aged 8 to 11 in England). In England (United Kingdom) and in Denmark, examples exist of national programmes which make it easy for primary schools to connect with people who are well placed to provide insights of value to children (Box 4.3).

Starting career guidance young will explicitly challenge stereotyping about the types of people who are suitable for different occupations and recognise the social contexts from which young people are drawn (CEDEFOP, 2017[21]; Musset and Mytna Kurekova, 2018[2]).

Each student need to receive pro-active and personalised guidance

Career guidance services need to be adequate and protected against the risk of being continuously squeezed at the margins of an activity such as regular teaching. Every student, whatever his/her personal background, needs to:

- Understand enough about career options to enable them to make informed decisions, whenever these decisions are open to them.

- Understand that choosing certain subjects and/or study programmes opens door to careers that would otherwise be closed.

- Understand enough about the world of work to know what skills, qualifications and attributes they need to succeed in it.

Career guidance services need to inform all young people of VET options alongside the other options available to them, therefore a discussion with career guidance professionals, where these options can be presented, need to be mandatory, and ideally sessions need to be regular (OECD, 2010[22]; Musset and Mytna Kurekova, 2018[2]).

Countries use diverse types of interventions, such as professional career counselling, assessments and tests, information provision and contacts with the world of education and the world of work. Specific interventions can target groups of students who may need more help in making career choices. These approaches are complementary and in many countries students benefit from a wide combination of them[4] (Musset and Mytna Kurekova, 2018[2]). Estonia already has many of these elements in place, but access to these services is uneven, and voluntary. Professional career counselling (one-on-one interviews with counsellors) should be compulsory in the run up of choosing a school and a track in grade 9. Career guidance needs to be more proactive and to target specific groups to overcome the barriers faced by students from under-represented groups. Schools and *Rajaleidja* agencies need to monitor participation.

Box 4.2. Interesting country practice in career guidance provision: Prince Edward Island in Canada

A comprehensive, all-encompassing multi-programme approach to career guidance has been developed by the Government of Prince Edward Island in Canada. It is based on a co-ordinated, whole school approach organised by career development themes. The key elements include: career development integrated into health education in grades 1-9; compulsory career course in grade 10; experiential learning opportunities through wide range of courses and programmes offered by the communities in school and including hands-on experience out-of-school; partnership with post-secondary institutions, employment specialist and industry sectors; specialised training to career guidance staff and teachers; parent/guardian coaching programme; and student graduation and transition planner based on four step inquiry process linking interests and skill, support networks, labour market information and post-secondary education options.

Source: ICCDPP (2015[23]), *Promising/Best Practices: Canada*, www.is2015.org/wp-content/uploads/2015/06/Canada-Promising-Practices-Panel-2-2.pdf.

Mandatory provision tackles unspoken assumptions

By making career guidance mandatory, an opportunity will emerge to ensure that the unspoken assumptions that young people have about vocational education can be challenged. Requiring student participation is likely to be of greatest benefit to young people from disadvantaged backgrounds. As teenagers, such young people are more likely to express confusion in career aspirations (Yates et al., 2010[24]). While ensuring that all young people receive a minimum level of guidance, schools should ensure that those young people who have most to gain from career guidance receive appropriate levels, even if above any entitlement. Such young people are likely to be from lower SES backgrounds and lacking family-based social networks which commonly enable easy access to reliable information concerning jobs and careers (Musset and Mytna Kurekova, 2018[2]; Mann, Rehill and Kashefpakdel, 2018[25]). It is essential that all young people are informed of the VET offer, and have the opportunity to visit VET schools and meet with people who work in occupations to which a VET education is a common gateway. Once in a VET programme, it is important that high quality career guidance continues, to ensure that students remain confident in their choice and are supported in thinking about future progression.

> **Box 4.3. Connecting the world of work with the schools from an early age**
>
> **The Route to VET**
>
> In Denmark, VET students act as role models and visit primary and lower secondary schools to raise awareness of vocational education. The Route to VET campaign was initiated and is led by the Danish VET Student Union. At the school visit, the young role models present their own experiences on why they chose VET, their training and the possibilities anticipated in both the labour market and for further education.
>
> *Source*: EEO, (2017[26]), *Kampagnen*, http://eeo.dk/vejentil/om-kampagnen/.
>
> **Primary Futures**
>
> In the United Kingdom, a project called Primary Futures, developed with the professional body representing primary school leaders (the National Association of Head Teachers) connects primary schools with the world of work by enabling schools to arrange visits from representatives of a broad range of occupations. Visits are arranged online and are designed to enable children see the relevance of what they learn at school and to challenge stereotypical thinking about jobs and careers. Through such experiences, it is anticipated that the children will become more motivated, better understanding how achievement at school relates to the possibilities that will open up for them later in life.
>
> *Source*: Education and Employers Taskforce (2018[27]) Primary Futures website, https://primaryfutures.org/.

Improve data in career provision and introduce destination surveys

Recommendation 4.2. Enhance use of data in career guidance, introducing destination surveys.

Labour market information can alter career decisions

In addition to advice and guidance from well-trained and impartial professionals in advance of grade 9, every student needs to have easy access to trustworthy labour market information. Evidence from Spain suggests that students take labour market information into account when making educational decisions, including the decision to drop out (Aparicio, 2010[28]). Evidence from France suggests that students do adjust their preferences in terms of field of study when they receive information about their future prospects (Hestermann and Pistolesi, 2016[29]).

Labour market information is available in Estonia

Estonia has made significant progress in collating labour market information (LMI) about current and future demand for labour and making that information available to guidance practitioners. Through the OSKA programme, data is gathered on important economic sectors. The *Rajaleidja* online portal includes a database of more than 200 jobs with descriptions outlining the nature of work, working conditions, knowledge, skills, personal qualities and education demanded, training and progression opportunities, salary and other benefits. Information is supplemented by videos (CEDEFOP, 2017[30]). While the availability of such data is important, it is used most effectively in the context of professional counselling. Practitioners, students and their families, moreover, need to be aware of such resources in user-friendly formats (CEDEFOP, 2016[31]).

Box 4.4. Destination surveys

Good quality data is essential to link educational provision to labour market needs, and it underpins career guidance. A destinations survey administered to those leaving vocational programmes around one year after completion, (or after they drop out) establishes whether graduates are working and in what occupation, whether they are pursuing further study, and if they are unemployed or otherwise not in the labour market. It can be undertaken through mobile phone contacts obtained from students, allowing a follow-up regardless of location. This allows the success or failure of different vocational programmes and institutions to be assessed. A survey can also ask graduates about what they thought of their vocational programme – whether it was well taught and provided them with relevant skills for example. In this way, such surveys also become a tool to monitor and improve quality. There is much international experience of destinations surveys, typically in higher education but also increasingly at secondary school level [as recommended by McCarthy and Musset (2016[32]), in the *Skills beyond School Review of Peru*].

In Australia the NCVER Student Outcomes Survey is conducted annually among students who completed some vocational training. Conducted by the National Centre for Vocational Education and Research since 1997, it is funded by the Australian government and provides information on employment and further study outcomes, the relevance and benefits of training, and student satisfaction. The information collected supports the administration, planning and evaluation of the VET system.

In Ireland, the School Leavers Survey is based on a national sample of school leavers, contacted 12 to 18 months after leaving school. Face-to-face interviews, used in this survey since its beginning in 1980, have become more difficult as a result of declining response rates and high costs. Therefore, from 2007 the Survey has used a mix of approaches. The selected individuals are asked to complete an online questionnaire, but could also ask for a paper copy. Participants are offered an incentive to complete the questionnaire, with their names being entered in a draw for prizes. Those who were particularly difficult to reach (e.g. early school leavers) were followed up by telephone initially and then face-to-face.

Source: OECD (2010[22]), *Learning for Jobs*, OECD Reviews of Vocational Education and Training, http://dx.doi.org/10.1787/9789264087460-en; McCarthy, M. and P. Musset (2016[32]), *Skills beyond School Review of Peru*, OECD Reviews of Vocational Education and Training, http://dx.doi.org/10.1787/9789264265400-en.

More use might be made of destination surveys

For LMI to have its greatest effect, it needs to be a resource which young people can make use of within their own highly personalised decision-making. LMI enriched by first-hand encounters with the labour market through employer engagement enables young people to make the fullest sense of the available statistics. In this context, it is important that they are given opportunity to understand what happens to students like them following particular programmes of study once they enter the working world. Here, the case for destination surveys (Box 4.4) is strong. Such information and guidance can also be used to fight gender stereotypes as women tend to be under-represented in some areas where labour market outcomes are strong.

Make sure that students interact with people in work and experience different workplaces

Recommendation 4.3. Make sure that students get multiple opportunities to interact with people in work and workplaces.

Direct experience of the workplace is essential within effective career guidance

Research evidence highlights the importance of career guidance being designed in a manner to enable students to gain a realistic insight into the demands of different occupations. This provides experiential information which enables more informed decision-making about education and job paths as students progress through education and training systems (Hughes et al., 2016[1]; Mann, Rehill and Kashefpakdel, 2018[25]). Direct experience of the workplace, and the engagement of employers, is therefore essential. As noted above, due to the devolved decision-making within Estonian schools, while there is a strong history of employer engagement in Estonia, it is not certain whether enough of these meaningful interactions between schools and work places are provided to young people.

Engaging people in work within career guidance activities

A 2018 international literature review provides a checklist for understanding the effective characteristics of employer engagement within career guidance. The study argues that volumes matters, with a number of studies highlighting the importance of at least four encounters with people in work across schooling. These opportunities to interact with people in work also need to be varied, and personalised: evidence suggests that deficit models should be applied and young people entering educational experiences with limited access to relevant work-related networks should be targeted with more intense interventions (Mann, Rehill and Kashefpakdel, 2018[25]).

While a wide range of employer engagement activities can enrich career thinking, career talks (as described in Box 4.5), job fairs, workplace visits and episodes of job shadowing are held in particularly high value (Musset and Mytna Kurekova, 2018[2]). In the Estonian context, the opportunity exists to systemise the engagement of employers in career guidance.

Box 4.5. Looking at the impact of career talks using longitudinal data

Kashefpakdel and Percy (2016[33]) analyse the British Cohort Study (1970) longitudinal dataset, designed to survey approximately 17 000 babies born in Great Britain, and use data from 1986 and 1996. At age 16, individuals were asked whether they had school-organised contacts with employers outside of school. Among respondents, receiving a career talk from speakers outside school was the most common, with 66% of students participating in at least one such talk. The survey also indicated how many of these talks from a speaker outside of school the individual has received in year 10 and year 11 (respectively aged 14-15 and 15-16).

The study tests for relationships between school-mediated career talks with speakers from outside of the school at ages 14-16 and full-time earnings at age 26. Extensive controls include family and social background, learning environment, and prior attainment. Looking at net weekly incomes at age 26, the analysis provides a test, therefore, as to whether wage premiums observed by young British adults with higher levels of teenage school-mediated workplace exposure might best be understood through social capital theory: that access to higher volume non-redundant, trusted information and insight about the job market through encounters with working professionals can be seen to provide economic advantages in later job market transitions. The study finds that at age 14-15 participation each career talk is associated with an earning premium, at age 26, of 0.8% (rising to 1.6% where the teenager reported their career talks to have been "very helpful"). The hypothesis they test is that each additional career talk will be associated with an additional change in outcomes, since each outside speaker will convey different insights. The authors also took into account how useful the students reported the talk to be, as an estimate of its quality.

Source: Kashefpakdel, E. and C. Percy (2016[33]), "Career education that works: An economic analysis using the British Cohort Study", *Journal of Education and Work*, Vol. 30/3, pp. 217-234, https://doi.org/10.1080/13639080.2016.1177636.

Notes

[1] The great majority of other studies considered revealed evidence of mixed or negligible outcomes.

[2] Iannelli and Smyth (2008[34]) use EU Labour Force Survey data on school-to-work transitions in several European countries (although not in Estonia) and show that in Eastern European countries, in particular socio-economic background, has a significant influence on education decisions.

[3] For example, in Ida-Virumaa (where Russians are mainly located after the Tallinn area) is historically an industrial and mining area. Also three strong VET schools (now united into one) are located in Ida-Virumaa, which also might affect the decisions and attractiveness of VET.

[4] In practice, identity development at pre-primary and primary levels of education can be organised in the form of co-operative activities or extracurricular activities that help children play roles and assume responsibilities. During secondary education, psychometric assessments, interest inventories, portfolios, action planning or personal development planning can also be used as frameworks for reflection.

References

Aparicio, A. (2010), "High-school dropouts and transitory labor market shocks: The case of the Spanish housing boom", *Discussion Paper*, No. 5139. [28]

Archer, L. et al. (2013), *ASPIRES Report: Young People's Science and Career Aspirations, Age 10 –14*, King's College London, London. [16]

CEDEFOP (2017), *"Guidance: supporting youth to manage their careers"*, http://www.cedefop.europa.eu/en/toolkits/vet-toolkit-tackling-early-leaving/intervene/intervention-approaches/guiding-young-people-make-right-choices. [21]

CEDEFOP (2017), *Case Study Visit Focusing on the "Pathfinder" Initiative, Estonia*, http://www.cedefop.europa.eu/files/5555_en_case_study_estonia.pdf. [30]

CEDEFOP (2016), *Labour Market Information and Guidance*, Publications Office of the European Union, Luxembourg, http://www.cedefop.europa.eu/files/5555_en.pdf. [31]

Department for Education (2017), *Careers Strategy: Making the Most of Everyone's Skills and Talents*, https://www.gov.uk/government/publications/careers-strategy-making-the-most-of-everyones-skills-and-talents. [19]

Education and Employers Taskforce (2018), *Primary Futures website*, https://primaryfutures.org/ (accessed on 20 November 2018). [27]

Erhvervsskolernes ElevOrganisation (EEO) (2017), *Kampagnen*, (Campaigns), http://eeo.dk/vejentil/om-kampagnen/. [26]

Flisi, S. et al. (2016), "Measuring occupational mismatch: Overeducation and overskill in Europe - Evidence from PIAAC", *Social Indicators Research*, Vol. 131/3, pp. 1211-1249, http://dx.doi.org/10.1007/s11205-016-1292-7. [6]

Foundation Innove (2018), *Lifelong Guidance in Estonia*, https://www.innove.ee/en/ (accessed on 6 June 2018). [13]

Foundation Innove (2018), *Qualifications of Guidance Practitioners*, https://www.innove.ee/en/ (accessed on 6 June 2018). [14]

Hestermann, N. and N. Pistolesi (2016), "Does the Provision of Information on their Skills Affect Students' Enrollment Choices?", *TSE Working Paper*, No. 16-650, Toulouse, France. [29]

Howard, K. et al. (2015), "Perceived influences on the career choices of children and youth: An exploratory study", *International Journal for Educational and Vocational Guidance*, Vol. 15/2, pp. 99-111, http://dx.doi.org/10.1007/s10775-015-9298-2. [18]

Hughes, D. et al. (2016), *Careers Education: International Literature Review*, Education Endowment Foundation. [1]

Iannelli, C. and E. Smyth (2008), "Mapping gender and social background differences in education and youth transitions across Europe", *Journal of Youth Studies*, Vol. 11/2. [34]

ICCDPP (2015), *Promising/Best Practices: Canada*, http://www.is2015.org/wp-content/uploads/2015/06/Canada-Promising-Practices-Panel-2-2.pdf. [23]

ILO (2016), *Non-standard Employment Around the World: Understanding Challenges, Shaping Prospects*, International Labor Organization, Geneva, https://www.ilo.org/wcmsp5/groups/public/---dgreports/---dcomm/---publ/documents/publication/wcms_534326.pdf. [3]

Kashefpakdel, E. and C. Percy (2016), "Career education that works: An economic analysis using the British Cohort Study", *Journal of Education and Work*, Vol. 30/3, pp. 217-234, https://doi.org/10.1080/13639080.2016.1177636. [33]

Kemppainen, R. and S. Ferrin Ellis (2002), "Parental choice and language-of-instruction policies and practices in Estonia", *Education and Urban Society*, Vol. 35/1, pp. 76-9. [11]

Lindemann, K. and E. Saar (2012), "Ethnic inequalities in education: second-generation Russians in Estonia", *Ethnic and Racial Studies*, Vol. 35/11, pp. 1974-1998, http://dx.doi.org/10.1080/01419870.2011.611890. [8]

Mägi, E. and M. Nestor (2012), *Koolilõpetajad ja nende karjäärivalikud*, (Graduates and Career Choices), Praxis, Tellija SA Archimedes ja Haridus- ja Teadusministeerium, http://www.praxis.ee/wp-content/uploads/2014/03/2012-Koolilopetajad-ja-nende-karjaarivalikud.pdf. [10]

Mann, A., J. Rehill and E. Kashefpakdel (2018), *Employer Engagement in Education: Insights from International Evidence for Effective Practice and Future Research*, Education Endowment Foundation, London. [25]

McCarthy, M. and P. Musset (2016), *A Skills beyond School Review of Peru*, OECD Reviews of Vocational Education and Training, OECD Publishing, Paris, http://dx.doi.org/10.1787/9789264265400-en. [32]

Ministry of Education and Research (2017), *Background Report for OECD on Vocational Education and Training (VET) in Estonia*, http://www.hm.ee/sites/default/files/uuringud/oecd_vet_background.pdf. [5]

Ministry of Education and Research (2014), *The Estonian Lifelong Learning Strategy 2020*, https://www.hm.ee/sites/default/files/estonian_lifelong_strategy.pdf. [15]

Musset, P. and L. Mytna Kurekova (2018), "Working it out: Career guidance and employer engagement", *OECD Education Working Papers*, No. 175, OECD Publishing, Paris, http://dx.doi.org/10.1787/51c9d18d-en. [2]

Neary, S., V. Hooley and T. Dodd (2015), *Understanding Career Management Skills: Findings From the First Phase of the CMS Leader Project*, International Centre for Guidance Studies, University of Derby. [4]

OECD (2017), *OECD Economic Surveys: Estonia 2017*, OECD Publishing, Paris, http://dx.doi.org/10.1787/eco_surveys-est-2017-en. [12]

OECD (2017), "Unemployment rates by age", *OECD.Stat*, https://stats.oecd.org (accessed on 18 September 2017). [7]

OECD (2010), *Learning for Jobs*, OECD Reviews of Vocational Education and Training, OECD Publishing, Paris, http://dx.doi.org/10.1787/9789264087460-en. [22]

Pärtel, K. and K. Petti (2013), *Kutsehariduse maine*, (The Reputation of Vocational Education), Innove, Tallinn, http://www.innove.ee/et/kutseharidus/programmidja-projektid/uuringud/kutsehariduse-maine-2013. [9]

Wade, P. et al. (2011), *Key Stage 2 Career-Related Learning Pathfinder Evaluation*, Department for Education, https://www.gov.uk/government/publications/key-stage-2-career-related-learning-pathfinder-evaluation. [20]

Watson, M. and M. McMahon (2005), "Children's career development: A research review from a learning perspective", *Journal of Vocational Behaviour* 67, pp. 119-132. [17]

Yates, S. et al. (2010), "Early occupational aspirations and fractured transitions: A study of entry into 'NEET' status in the UK", *Journal of Social Policy*, Vol. 40/03, pp. 513-534, http://dx.doi.org/10.1017/s0047279410000656. [24]

ORGANISATION FOR ECONOMIC CO-OPERATION AND DEVELOPMENT

The OECD is a unique forum where governments work together to address the economic, social and environmental challenges of globalisation. The OECD is also at the forefront of efforts to understand and to help governments respond to new developments and concerns, such as corporate governance, the information economy and the challenges of an ageing population. The Organisation provides a setting where governments can compare policy experiences, seek answers to common problems, identify good practice and work to co-ordinate domestic and international policies.

The OECD member countries are: Australia, Austria, Belgium, Canada, Chile, the Czech Republic, Denmark, Estonia, Finland, France, Germany, Greece, Hungary, Iceland, Ireland, Israel, Italy, Japan, Korea, Latvia, Lithuania, Luxembourg, Mexico, the Netherlands, New Zealand, Norway, Poland, Portugal, the Slovak Republic, Slovenia, Spain, Sweden, Switzerland, Turkey, the United Kingdom and the United States. The European Union takes part in the work of the OECD.

OECD Publishing disseminates widely the results of the Organisation's statistics gathering and research on economic, social and environmental issues, as well as the conventions, guidelines and standards agreed by its members.

OECD PUBLISHING, 2, rue André-Pascal, 75775 PARIS CEDEX 16
(91 2019 03 1 P) ISBN 978-92-64-31308-8 – 2019

Printed by Libri Plureos GmbH in Hamburg,
Germany